MW00617607

CENTEN

BATTLESHIP OREGON IS VICTORIOUS
AT BATTLE OF SANTIAGO DE CUBA

—CENTENNIAL JULY 3, 1998—
—MEDFORD, OREGON 97501—

𝕷imited 𝕰dition
T h i s   I s   C o p y

No. 414 of 1,000
Copies Printed

The *Oregon* (1896-1956) is the only American battleship to serve in these three wars:
The Spanish-American War
First World War
World War II

American Major Fighting Ships That Participated in Naval Battle of Santigao de Cuba July 3, 1898
(Including Battleship *Maine*)

Sister ships:
Indiana,
Massachusetts,
Oregon

Name	Keel laid	Commsnd	Off men	Armament (large)	Tubes	Armor	Dimensions / displ	Speed	H.P.	Engines	Notes
Texas	1 Ju 89	15 Au 95	30 362	(2) 12"; (2) 6"; (12) 6 pdr.	(4) 14"	12"	308'10" X 64'1" X 6,311	17	8,600	Vertical 3-expansion reciprical	1.
Maine	17 Oc 88	17 Se 95	31 343	(4) 10"; (6) 3) 6"; (7) 6 pdr.	-do-	12"	319' x 57' x 6,682	17	6,000	-do-	2.
Indiana (BB-1)	7 Ma 91	20 No 95	32 441	(4) 13"; (8) 8"; (20) 6 pdr.	(4) 18'	18"	350'11" x 69'3" x 10,288	15	9,000	-do-	3.
Massachusetts (BB-2)	25 Jn 91	10 Jn 96	32 441	-do-	-do-	-do-	-do-	15	9,000	-do-	4.
Oregon (BB-3)	19 Jn 91	15 Jy 96	32 441	-do-	-(6)-	-do-	-do-	15	9,000	-do-	5.
Iowa (BB-4)	5 Au 93	16 Jn 97	36 450	-do-	(4) 14"	15"	3625" x 723" x 11,410	15	11,000	-do-	6.

Notes:-
1. Last commissioned 11 Fe 1911. (Name changed to San Marcos) 16 Fe 1911. Sunk–gunnery practice 20 Mr 1911
2. Destroyed by internal explosion Havana, Cuba 15 Fe 1898. Hulk salvaged 1911-1912; sunk in Straits of Florida 16 Mr 1912
3. Last commissioned 31 Mr 1919. Name changed to Battleship No. 1 (BB-1). 29 Mr 1919. Sunk as bomb target 1 Nv 1920
4. 31 Mr 1919. Name changed to Coast Battleship No. 2 (BB-2), 29 Mr 1919. Struck from list Nv. 1920. Sunk as Army Artillery target
5. Designated Battleship No. 3 (BB-3) 29 Mr 1919. De-militarized 4 Ja 1924 loaned to State of Oregon as Memorial. Redesignated (XI-22).
   Sold for scrapping 7 De 1942. Reacquired by U.S.N. Se 1943. Hull used as barge for dynamite, other items, towed to
   Marshall Islands then Guam 1944. Sold at Guam for scrapping in Japan 15 Mr 1956. See photo on page 116.
6. Last commissioned 31 Mr 1920. Name changed to Coast Battleship No. 4 (BB-4). 29 Mr 1919. Sunk as gunnery target 22 Mr 1923

BATTLESHIP OREGON

BULLDOG OF THE NAVY

SPANISH-AMERICAN WAR CENTENNIAL (1898 - 1998) COMMEMORATIVE EDITION

DOCUMENTARY BY BERT WEBBER

WEBB RESEARCH GROUP PUBLISHERS

Published by
WEBB RESEARCH GROUP
Books About the Oregon Country
P. O. Box 314
Medford, Oregon 97501

Library of Congress Cataloging In Publications Data

Webber, Bert
    Battleship Oregon : bulldog of the Navy : documentary / by Bert
Webber. – Spanish-American War centennial (1898-1998) commemorative ed.
      p.   cm.
    Includes bibliographical references and index.
    ISBN 0-936738-24-3
    1. Oregon (Battleship) 2. Spanish-American War, 1898–Campaigns–
Cuba. 3. Spanish-American War, 1898–Naval operations, American. I. Title
    VA65.07W43 1998   98-15985
    973.8'95 — dc21   CIP

Contents

Dedication	7
Introduction	9
1. Cause of the Spanish-American War	13
2. The Voyage of the Ages	17
3. Historic Battle of Santiago de Cuba	47
4. Return to the Pacific	63
5. Philippine Adventure	67
6. Asiatic Patrols and Troubles	69
7. West Coast Patrols	77
8. Interim Duty	83
9. The Orient Again	84
10. First World War	86
11. Post-War Doldrums Then a Grand Review	87
12. Oregon's Floating Monument	91
13. World War II – Guam	109
14. The Battleship *Oregon's* Post Office	117

Appendices:

A.	Commanding Officers 1896 – 1919	122
B.	Naval and Marine Officers On Board During Battle of Santiago de Cuba	123
C.	The Crew on Board During Battle of Santiago de Cuba	124
D.	United States Marines on Board During Battle of Santiago de Cuba	129
E.	Commendation by the Bureau of Steam Navigation	130
F.	A Short Biography of Rear Admiral Charles E. Clark	131
G.	Affect of the Washington Naval Conference on Limitations of Weapons on the Battleship *Oregon*	134

About the Author	135
Bibliography	137
Illustration credits	138
Index	139

Battle-scarred battleship *Oregon* immediately after the Battle of Santiago de Cuba

This book is fondly dedicated to our eldest son

Richard E. Webber

Even as a youngster, he loved the water. He rigged a rented row boat with a bed sheet for a sail and cruised at Alta Lake State Park, Washington. Later, as an electronic technician in the Coast Guard, he followed the route of the battleship *Oregon* in the icebreaker *USCGC Eastwind* along the west coast of South America and put in at Callao, Peru. On the same voyage, he circumnavigated Antarctica as part of Operation Deep Freeze (1967). Next, as did the *Oregon,* Rick transited the Strait. of Magellan and visited Punta Arenas. Later that year, on the *Eastwind,* he cruised the Barents and Kara Seas and would have transited the North East Passage to Alaska but Soviet clearance was denied. Still an electronics technician, he transferred to *USCGC Cactus* for duty in the eastern Caribbean. Discharged after service at Nantucket's Siasconset Lighthouse in LORAN maintenance, he graduated as an Engineer (Nuclear Option) from Idaho State University and became a Nuclear Power Station safety engineer. For the Re-dedication of the Statue of Liberty ceremony, he took his small power boat through Verrazano Narrows and joined the tall ships sailing the Hudson River where *Oregon* paraded in 1898. Rick currently does custom AutoCad design work and lives with his wife in Stratford, N.J. They have two grown children. He recently visited Seattle and said, "I'm really itchy to get a moving deck under my feet again," so he took a ride on the Mulikteo Ferry.

Very Sincerely yours
C.E. Clark.
Captain U.S.N.

Captain Charles E. Clark, U.S.N. at
his desk aboard the Battleship *Oregon*.

Introduction

At this writing, 100 years after the outstanding sea voyage of the Battleship *Oregon* where the ship "ran like a locomotive" through two oceans in record time, then fired the first and last shots in the defeat the Spanish Navy at the Battle of Santiago de Cuba, it is time to set down the historically accurate account of those events as well as little known factors that have come to light in recent years.

Most of those who study histories of battleships agree that the accomplishments of the *Oregon* make her the most distinguished battleship of all nations of all time.

The causes that led to the Spanish-American War are several, not the least being the untimely destruction of the Battleship *Maine* while anchored in the harbor of Havana. As pointed out in Admiral Rickover's book (see bibliography), "the possibility of war was imminent and the nation was clamoring for a report" about the sunken ship. A court, appointed by the president, in an obvious effort to seek a reason that did not make the U. S. Navy look bad, declared that the cause was an external explosion* apparently from a make-shift Spanish mine. As a result, the people's clamor for war was beaten into a frenzy in the "court of public opinion" – the newspapers – with master hucksters fanning the flames. The hype can surely be laid at the feet of William Randolph Hearst and Joseph Pulitzer. These men were giants among newspaperman who were fighting each other for increased circulation for their papers. More about these journalists in Chapter 1.

This book is a biography of the battleship *Oregon* from the decision to build the ship in 1893 until it was broken up for scrap

---

* In spite of the verdict of the court, there was quiet suspicion that the explosion had been inside the ship but this was not clearly established until other Boards of Inquiry investigated the catastrophe in 1911-1912. The final word: Probably a fire in bituminous coal in bunker A-16 caused by spontaneous combustion then explosions in that bunker spread to the magazines which then exploded and sank the *Maine.*

by the Japanese in 1956. This fighting ship played a key role in the Spanish-American War and it is the purpose here to tell about it. Further, for the era, *Oregon* (later designated BB3), was the only battleship to be in three wars – the Spanish-American War, the First World War as well as in World War II. Its role in each was completely different and we will identify them.

As far as the "Spanish War," as it's called, is concerned, this book restricts itself to the matters of the navy and specifically to the *Oregon,* but includes other ships when the *Oregon* worked with them. This book has a few other wartime and post-war activities to provide some depth. Many other actions, including Theodore Roosevelt's Rough Riders and the charge up San Juan Hill, details of the famous spy activities for the Americans by U. S. Army Lt. Andrew S. Rowan,* must be left to others.

The sources for this book are many. They started with the interview with Colonel Rowen in 1937. We looked at 1898 newspaper accounts, government documents, magazine articles and a host of books. The major references are in the bibliography.

> The letters "USS" on Navy ships was not official until President Theodore Roosevelt signed Exec. Order 549 on January 8, 1907. When launched, the *Oregon* was merely "Coast Battleship No. 3." Here, we use *Oregon* as well as *USS Oregon* to provide variety.

Some of the prime people who were involved with us in this project include Mary Tichenor Cooper. The Tichenors and the Coopers have long been associated with the sea and shared their experiences. She presented a copy of her mother's booklet to me which was used as the base from which to get started. Her mother, Mary Walker Tichenor, had privately published the booklet: *Dedicated to the Memory of All the Boys Who Sailed "The Seven Seas" on....The Battleship Oregon, The Bull Dog of the Navy* in 1937. This was followed by an expanded edition in 1942. It was sea-Captain William Tichenor (1813-1887), her grandfather, who landed the first men trying to found the town of Port Orford on the Oregon Coast in 1851. This deadly adventure

---

* Colonel Rowan, USA (retired), elderly and a permanent guest at Letterman General Hospital, Presidio of San Francisco, admonished, on the occasion of the author's visit with him in the late 1930's: "On land or sea where ever you are, always honor the flag and be prepared."

is recorded in our book *Battle Rock the Hero's Story...How a Small Canon Done Its Work....* Mary Tichenor Cooper was married to George Cooper, USCG, who in *Manana* on June 21, 1942, was the closest ship, by just a few hundred yards, to the Japanese submarine while it was shelling Fort Stevens, Oregon. His recollection of that incident is in our book *Silent Siege III, Japanese Attacks on North America in World War II.* I very much appreciate the Tichenor-Cooper interest and assistance with these projects.

Among the many tasks of professional reference librarians, who have vast resources immediately available, is to help locate data needed by the public. There are a number who were involved with the project. Anne Billeter, Ph.D., Head of Readers' Services which includes the Reference Department of the Jackson County Library, Medford, Oregon, and members of her staff, are never stinting in their willingness to help, I thank them. Richard Portal, Master Librarian retired, Salem, Oregon, helped with data at the State Library level that is not readily available locally. I thank him generously for his friendship and assistance.

Dean Allard, Ph.D., head of the Naval History Division, Washington, D.C. is a keen researcher, archivist and speaker. He has assisted with a number of our projects over the years including this one and I thank him again.

Mary Beth Straight, and her assistants at the United States Naval Institute, Annapolis, brought together their pictures of the battleship *Oregon* from which we made selections for this book. I am indebted to them for their willing assistance.

Admiral Tatsuo Tsukuduo, formerly of the Imperial Japanese Navy (WWII) and later the Japanese Maritime Self-Defense Force (retired), has been a friend and research colleague for many years. In WWII, he made three trips to the west coast of the U. S. as Executive Officer of submarine *I-25,* the aircraft-carrying submarine that caused particular havoc on its missions and earned a unique place in history due to its work – See *Silent Siege-III.*

Tsukuduo-san, a learned and articulate gentlemen as well as being the Chief Priest of the Navy Shrine, journeyed by train to Kure and located local newspaper accounts of the repair of the *Oregon* in the Navy Yard there in 1900. The ship had snagged

11

her bottom on a rock off China. We learned this was only a temporary fix observing that the Japanese really did not want a U.S. battleship in their dry-dock. Admiral Tsukuduo also located the last photographs and provided copies showing the *Oregon* in the hands of the Japanese ship-breakers. The materials he furnished have not appeared in any previous books. I am honored to have Admiral Tsukuduo as a collaborator for this project.

Locating data about the visit of President Woodrow Wilson to the battleship at Seattle in 1919 was challenging so I am indebted to Patricia A. Hobbs, Curator of Collections of Woodrow Wilson Birthplace, Staunton, Virginia for her willing assistance.

The presumption that there was a U. S. Post Office on the *Oregon* came about as the author was aware of post offices on other U. S. naval vessels. But data about the *Oregon's* postal history was elusive and would probably have remained so had it not been for the kind help of Dean Allard, who mentioned the Universal Ship Cancellation Society in New Britain, Connecticut. We corresponded with David A. Kent, who then mentioned James P. Myerson of Los Angeles. We were also able to reach Gilbert Pittman in Wichita, Kansas, Leonard Lukens of Phoenix, Oregon and John King in Sacramento. I thank these dedicated historians for input and for sending copies of rare postmarks.

Bridget E. Smith, a journalist and publisher of the *Historical Gazette*, Portland, Oregon, attended the 100th anniversary celebration of the launching of the *Oregon* when a reception was held at the Oregon Historical Society on October 23, 1993. Her input is appreciated.

While I have made every effort for completeness, and I am grateful to all those who have helped in even the smallest way, there may be something I did not discover that would make this story more complete. If this is so, readers with information are encouraged to write to me at the publisher listed on page *iv*.

Bert Webber
Central Point, Oregon

1. Cause of the Spanish-American War

Clouds of war were hovering over the United States and the people were growing more and more aroused to fury over the way the Spanish had treated the people of the little American-neighbor Island, Cuba. From the beginning of the Spanish control over Cuba, their rule was cruel and unjust. Revolution between the Cubans and Spain went on for several years during which time the Cuban insurgent army grew to more than 200,000.

American indignation grew more bitter as the struggle went on and they watched the uneven battle of the peace-loving people struggling against the old policies of Spain.

Trying to negotiate a peace, the United States sent one of our largest and most powerful battleships, the *Maine*, to the harbor of Havana where, on the night of February 15, 1898, she was suddenly blown up and 266 of her officers and men were killed in the explosion.

Great excitement swept over the United States. As we have seen, the President appointed a naval court which reported that the *Maine* had been blown up by the explosion of a submarine mine. But almost from the first, there was doubt, in some circles, that the explosion had been caused by a mine or by Spain.

Although President William McKinley did what he thought was best to bring settlement with Spain, reporters peppered their newspapers with extraordinary war-mongering stories. These headline-seeking journalists did their best to out-scream each other just to sell newspapers. Simply said, William Randolph Hearst wanted to build vast circulation for his New York *Journal* to beat the sales being made by the New York *World* owned by Joseph Pulitzer. But Hearst did not flinch at bending the truth. His flamboyant style with wild stories sold thousands of papers. Incredible as it seems, his sensationalism brought so much pressure on public officials that, in short, there seemed nothing left to do but for the United States to go to war. The United States was

U.S.S. *Maine* at anchor in harbor of Havana on July 2, 1898. (Lower) The *Maine*, sunk – sitting on the bottom of the harbor on July 3, 1898, but American flag still flys.

forced into an unnecessary war against Spain.* The U. S. declared war on April 21, 1898.

* Pressure on the President to declare war cannot all be heaped upon the heads of Hearst and Pulitzer for prominent Republicans as Assistant Secretery of the Navy Theodore Roosevelt, Senators Beveridge and Lodge as well as the Ambassador to Great Britain, John Hay, and others all had the President's ear. While Hearst boasted "How do you like the *Journal's* war,"(Editions of May 9, 10, 1898). Hay called it the "splendid little war." It was "little" in duration, only 4 months, but killed 5.462 Americans only 379 of them in battles.

Swanberg wrote:

It was an unnecessary war. It was the newspapermans' war. Above all, it was Hearst's war. It is safe to say that had not Hearst [and his *New York Journal*], with his magnificently tawdry flair for publicity and agitation, enlisted the women of America in a crusade they misunderstood ... made the *Maine* a mistaken symbol of Spanish treachery, caused thousands of citizens to write their Congressmen, and dragged the powerful *World* [Pulitzer's paper] along with him into journalistic ill-fame, the public would have kept its sanity, [President] McKinley would have shown more spunk ... and there would have been no war.

Did William Randolph Hearst cause the war just to sell newspapers? The headline of his *Evening Journal* on April 20, 1898 declared:

NOW TO AVENGE THE MAIN

At his own expense, amid great publicity in his own newspaper, he bought a ship, outfitted it and offered to pay the salaries of the crew, all to become part of the U.S. Navy to fight the Spaniards. He often, with his editorial staff, referred to the war as "our war." On the front pages of his papers appeared the query: "How Do You Like the *Journal's* War?"

The Spanish fleet, in and around the Havana Harbor, was made up of several very powerful ships. The Spaniards had no fear that the United States and believed it to have a small and inferior navy. The Spanish admiral was certain he could conquer the Cuban revolutionaries without any trouble from the U. S. Navy. But such proved not to be the case because the pride and the power and the glory of Spain was, within just a few short hours, piled up along the Cuban shore for miles. The *USS Oregon* had a very important part in the fray for which she received the plaudits of an admiring world. ✢

Poor Planning Doomed A Fleet

Admiral Cervera told Spanish authorities that to send a squadron across the Atlantic was to send it to its destruction. When he collected his ships and was ordered by Madrid to leave for the West Indies, he did so without a reserve force or supplies. He had indefinite instructions and no port of destination. He was without a plan of campaign.

U.S.S. Oregon in the orient

2. The Voyage of the Ages

The history of the United States would not be complete without the heroic, historic, and romantic stores from the records of the Navy. While there are hundreds of anecdotes that relate to all of the ships of the Navy, three ships are singled out for mention here. These are the *USS Constitution* ("Old Ironsides") the cruiser *Olympia* and the battleship *Oregon*. Each have been set apart as shrines for their country's patriotic thoughts and visits. "Old Ironsides" is berthed at the Boston Navy Yard. The *Olympia* is home on the Delaware River at Philadelphia. For many years the battleship *Oregon* was a floating monument visited by thousands every year, until the beginning of World War II, in the Willamette River at Portland, Oregon.

The *Constitution* remains in commission as the nation's most symbolic relic of the War of 1812. The *Olympia,* Admiral George Dewey's flagship in the Battle of Manila Bay, is maintained and cared for by a private historical foundation. Alas, the *Oregon,* the star of the battle of Santiago de Cuba, is no more. This battleship (10,288 tons displacement), truly a great ship for its time but dwarfed by World War II era battleships (45,000 tons displacement), was recalled for World War II duty. We will discuss this in chapter 13.

During the twenty years succeeding the Civil War, nothing had been done to build up or maintain the American Navy. The ships afloat during the Civil War had either been disposed of or had gradually become useless through age, hence to all intents and purposes the people of the United States had no Navy. In 1883, Congress authorized the building of four steel cruisers and from that time on the Navy grew. Cruisers and battleships of great strength and speed were the result.

In the spring of 1890, General B. F. Tracy, Secretary of the Navy, succeeded in getting an appropriation for three battleships afterwards named *Indiana, Massachusetts* and *Oregon*. Congress ordered the building of these vessels June 30, of which

$3,180,000 was appropriated for the building of the *Oregon*.

When the contracts were let, the building of two of these vessels went to Cramp's Shipyard on the Atlantic coast and one, the *Oregon*, to the Union Iron Works of San Francisco, California. Irving Scott, of the firm, was the chief builder.

The Bethlehem Iron Works at South Bethlehem, Pennsylvania, made for the *Oregon*:

> 72.07 tons of engine forgings
> 750.80 tons of armor plate
> 346 tons of gun forgings
> This totaled 1,168.87 tons of forgings.

The keel of the battleship *Oregon* was laid November 19, 1891 with great ceremony. On October 13, 1892, a small model of the ship was put on exhibition in the *Oregonian* section of the Great Industrial Fair in Portland, Oregon. Miss Iva Barker christened the model. After she dipped her fingers into a bowl of champagne, she sprinkled the glass case in which the model rested and declared:

> On behalf of the State of which we are proud, I name thee *Oregon*.

Work on the ship continued for two years. When launching time came, engraved invitations were distributed.

At the top of the invitation was a small engraving of the battleship. *

A little before noon on Oct. 26, 1893, the battleship *Oregon*, the first of her class to be constructed on the Pacific Coast, was launched from the Union Iron Works, San Francisco, in the presence of one of the largest crowds ever assembled there to witness such events. The sponsor at the launching was Miss Daisy Ainsworth, daughter of Captain J. C. Ainsworth, president of the Oregon Steam Navigation Company.

Representatives of the Navy and Army, civil officials of the general government and of the States of California and Oregon were present. Quite a party of Oregonians were there as special guests of the builder. The shipyard was filled with invited guests, while every available place on streets, wharves, buildings and

---

* The type style used here is different than on original invitation as similar type was not located.

Christened by
Miss Daisy Ainsworth
representing the State of Oregon
and

Launched by
Miss Eugenia Shelby
representing the City of Portland

Miss Ruth Dolph
representing the Navy

The pleasure of your company is requested to witness the launch
of the
Armored Coast Line Battleship
"Oregon"
Thursday, October 26th, 1893, at 11:46 A.M.

Union Iron Works

Present at gate

surrounding hills where ever a view point might be had of the
works, was filled by thousands of enthusiastic, patriotic spec-
tators. It was a great day in San Francisco.

General H. B. Compson, a Civil War Veteran from Portland,
represented Gov. Sylvester Pennoyer of Oregon. At three minutes
of twelve o'clock the last chock was knocked away by workmen.
At a given signal, Miss Eugenia Shelby, the great grand-daughter
of General Joseph Lane, the first territorial governor of Oregon,
representing the City of Portland, pressed the electric button
which started the brightly decorated ship down the ways. At the
same time, her escort, General Compson, said:

On behalf of Governor Pennoyer and the people of Oregon, I bid thee God
speed. Guard well thy name, The *Oregon*

Great in war and peace and in the history of the developing
United States, the State of Oregon gave an honored name to the
new battleship.

19

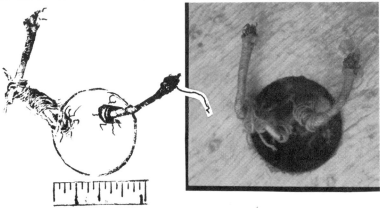

The "electric button" pushed by Miss Eugenia Shelby to launch the *USS Oregon* is in the lower left corner of the oil painting by E. Penez. The painting was commissioned expressly for this ceremony. During construction, a 1-inch diameter hole was drilled through the painting which was done on a solid board 15/16ths-inch thick. An ordinary electric push button was mounted in the hole. Looking at the back of the painting, one finds short stubs of two wires. These wires are pre-20th century-type stranded copper covered with nearly hair-thin silk thread insulation wound around each wire. This pair of wires ran an undetermined distance from the painting which is presumed to have been on an easel as shown here. As Miss Shelby pushed the button, the electric current operated a small guillotine that cut the final rope holding the ship thus the vessel was launched. The color photograph on the cover of this book was made directly from this painting.

20

It was not until July 31, 1896, that the battleship was completed and placed in commission. In all, the cost was $6,380,000. The ship was capable of 16.79 knots per hour with a contract speed of 15 knots. The estimated horse power developed by the engines was 9,000. For every quarter knot by which she exceeded the contract speed, the builders were to receive a bonus of $25,000. For every quarter knot by which she fell below the contract, a penalty of $25,000 was to be paid to the government.

On her sea trials, she maintained an average of 16.79 knots and the engines indicated 11,111 horsepower, or 2,111 in excess of the engineering estimate. The ship was rated to carry 32 officers, 441 sailors and a company of 60 marines. This is 553 at full complement.

The rudder was the largest forging ever made on the west coast to that time. It was as big as two barn doors measuring fifteen feet in width and sixteen feet in height. It was seventeen inches thick at the stock. It could be steered from four different locations in widely separate parts of the ship.

The *Oregon's* largest guns shot 13-inch projectiles each weighing over a half ton. The total weight of a volley from the four big guns was 4,400 pounds. Compared with the Spanish cruisers, this 4,000 pounds was the total weight of all eight of the shells from the 10-inch guns making up the main batteries of each of the four Spanish ships.*

The disparity in trained ability and general seamanship was even greater.

Other specifications:

Deck plates, 3-inches thick with gun position protection varying from 3 to 17-inches

2 3-inch field guns on carriages	4, 18-inch torpedo tubes
4 13-inch 35-caliber main turret guns	Mean normal draft: 22.4-feet
8 8-inch 35 caliber guns	Length (waterline): 348-feet
12 3-inch guns (Apparently installed about 1906)	Overall length: 351 feet
20 6-pounder guns	Beam 69-feet 3-inches
4 4-pounder guns	Armor belt, 18-inches
4 6-inch guns (replaced by 3-inch rapid fire in 1906-1907)	

---

* In the port-side photograph aboard the *Maria Teresa*, it will be observed that the ship's guns are without breech blocks. It is suspected but unclear if the ship put to sea without these guns being operational, or if the U. S. Navy prize crew took them off. In September, The *Maria Teresa* was raised by U. S. Navy and towed to Guantanamo Bay.

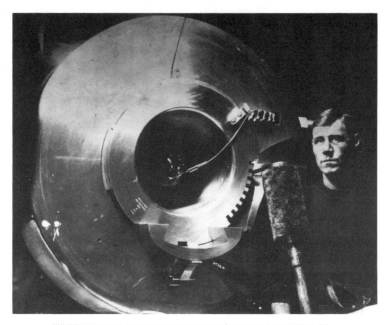

Aboard the *Oregon.* Gunner at the breech of one of the 13" guns. (Lower) Engine room of the battleship.

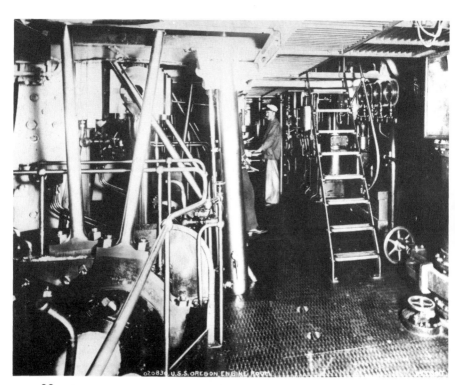

The *Oregon's* power plant was two, triple-expansion reciprocal engines with twin screws capable of driving the vessel through the water at better than 16 knots. But she was built for only fifteen knots under service conditions. It is important to keep these speed numbers in mind for they proved of great importance later in the running battle.

For the power plant: There were 4 fire-tubed boilers with 4 (double-ended) furnaces each fired from 8 rooms on the main line plus 2 fire-tubed single-ended (each with 3 furnaces) for the auxiliaries.

When the long run from San Francisco Bay to Jupiter Inlet in Florida was completed, it was officially stated that "not a bolt had started [loosened]." At the time of this battleship's completion, she was considered the sixth most formidable battleship in the world.

The Union Iron Works of San Francisco had already built several other vessels for the U. S. Navy among them the cruiser *Olympia*. But the *Oregon* was their first battleship. It had been their pride to make her as mechanically perfect as possible. For instance, when the installation of her condenser tubes had been completed, it was learned that those on the *Olympia*, which were of the same type, were not providing the best results. The managers of the Union Iron Works requested that the Navy return the cruiser and allow time to change the tubes in the *Olympia* at no cost to the government. This was done but the company paid out over $6,000 – a lot of money in 1896 – to do the work.

Captain Henry L. Howison was given the honor of being the first commander of the *Oregon*. His duty was from July 15, 1896 to March 20, 1897. Short sea trials were made to Monterey Bay in October and November 1896 then the ship was attached to the Pacific Squadron on December 28, 1896. Next the new battleship was ordered to make a test run to Acapulco, Mexico for a thorough trial of her sea-going qualities. She arrived at Acapulco on January 24, 1897. The return trip was started the same day with a stop for a week's target practice in Magdalene Bay, Baja California. The ship returned to San Francisco on February 16. Then she was ordered to the Straits of Juan De Fuca and Puget Sound.

On March 20, 1897, Captain A. S. Barker was ordered to

The Battleship *Oregon* in San Francisco Bay. The bridge had been finished in polished mahogany but just before the battle at Santiago, all this beautiful woodwork was carefully removed as a precaution against fire should the ship be hit during the fighting. Compare with picture on page *vi*. Although there were 45 states at this time, the ship had only a 44-star flag.

The official silver service for the ship was paid for with donations from Oregon citizens. It is preserved at the Oregon Historical Society.

command the ship. In June of that year, the *Oregon* went to Esquimalt, British Columbia to represent the American government at the Golden Jubilee Anniversary of the reign of Queen Victoria of England.

Returning to Seattle on July 6, 1897, the ship was placed in the dry dock for inspection and overhaul. Captain Barker and his officers proceeded to Portland where the $25,000 thirty-piece silver punch set was presented to the Officers to be placed upon the state's name-sake, the Battleship O*regon.*

The school children of the state were given the honor of raising this sum by donation of no more than 10-¢ each. Adults could put in only 25¢ each person. The contributions rolled in from all parts of the state and soon the order for making the set awarded to The Feldenhelmers, Silversmiths in Portland.

The service consisted of the large bunch bowl, a dipper and a slop bowl to hold the dipper, large tray and twenty-four silver holders for the twenty-four crystal clear glasses. Every piece is precisely engraved, the principal design being the Beaver. On the side of the punch bowl is engraved the legend:

From The
Citizens Of The State Of Oregon
To The
U. S. Battleship "Oregon"
1896

This magnificent silver service, secured by citizens of the state as a testimonial to the battleship *Oregon*, was presented by Governor William Paine Lord, on behalf of the people, to Captain Albert S. Barker, Commanding the battleship, and representing the officers and men of the ship, on July 6, 1897.

Multnomah Field was the place chosen for the presentation but on account of it being a rainy day, the ceremony was moved into the Armory.

The silver service was conspicuously placed on a large table resting amid the folds of an American Flag. Encircling the table were ranged the representatives of the Navy, and other military as well as servants of the state and city.

The monitor *Monterey,* commanded by Captain Charles E. Clark, and her sister ship the *Monadnock* were lying in Portland's harbor. A conspicuous feature of the ceremony were 200 crisp appearing sailors from these vessels.

Chairman Dodd, of the General Committee, introduced Governor Lord. His presentation speech was responded to by Captain Barker who accepted the service on behalf of the government and the officers and men of the *Oregon.*

After the silver service was carefully packed and ready to carry to Seattle, the floor was cleared and the 200 sailors presented a precision exhibition drill.

Until the beginning of 1898, the *Oregon* patrolled the Pacific Coast of the United States and the ship was dubbed the "Pacific Fleet" of the Navy. During these cruises, it was determined that

The *Oregon* on sea trials off the coast near San Francisco. The ship's guns had not yet been mounted.

Photography Can Be Risky

On account of the wide beam and somewhat blunt bow of a battleship, it rolls up a great wave when the ship moves at high speed. It occurred to an enterprising photographer, Mr. O. V. Lange, that the great on-rushing ship with its bow smothered in a mass of boiling water (page 27-lower) would make a great picture. Arrangements were made with the captain of a tug boat to steam directly across the *Oregon's* bow as she came at full speed – a plan the *Oregon's* commander was not told.

The vessels were almost together when the tug was seen from the battleship moving directly across its course. It was too late for the great ship to swerve on whose stem a foaming wave was piling nearly 12-feet high and spreading far on each side. The *Oregon* seemed about to bear directly down upon the tug where great consternation was growing. The cameraman later declared:

The *Oregon* seemed to be coming like a cannon ball but I was determined to get the picture even if it was my last. I steadied my nerves, looked into the view-finder and clicked the shutter. Then, with the camera under one arm, I jumped to a stanchion and held on for dear life.

In the next moment, he said there was a roar of rushing water and a violent whirling and pitching of the little tug which escaped collision by the fraction of a second as the *Oregon* flashed by within a few feet.

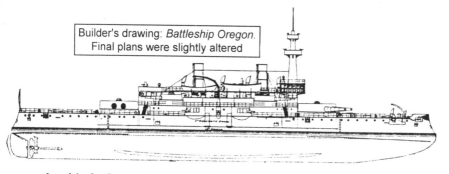

the ship had a tendency to roll even though she was never called upon to show her full strength and speed.

In the fall of 1897, authorization was received for the installation of rolling chocks and bilge keels that would increase stability in a heavy sea. The ship was ordered to the then new Puget Sound Navy Yard at Bremerton, Washington, where the work was done in what is now known as Dry Dock No. 1.

The huge ship, now in command of Captain Alexander Mc-Cormick, was coming out of dry dock on Feb. 16, 1898 when the startling news was flashed of the destruction of the battleship *Maine* in the harbor of Havana, Cuba. The officers and men were horrified with the reports. Gradually they drew together in small groups recalling names of friends who had been assigned to the *Maine* and of the strange disaster that had just destroyed her. Although the *Maine* was one of the nation's largest battleships, the new *Oregon* was heavier. This incident had happened in a friendly harbor.

With war eminent, the men believed they would become involved. The newspapers, particularly the *Post-Intelligencer* (the Hearst paper in Seattle), were full of war-mongering. There seemed little doubt that the 2-year-old battleship *Oregon* would have a part in it. Because the papers were blaming Spain for the disaster, it did not take long for an *esprit de corps* to arouse a longing within the sailors to avenge their comrades lost on the *Maine.* Grasping at possibilities, they realized that the *Oregon,* just out of dry dock, could not be in better shape to sail to any part of the globe at high speed.

In a very few hours, after receiving orders from Washington, the ship was on the way out of Puget Sound to go back to San Francisco.

On arrival there, sealed orders were received on March 19 to proceed to Callao, Peru. Everyone was happy and work went on rapidly night and day, taking on board 1,600 tons of coal; 500 tons of ammunition and stores and provisions to last six months.

In San Francisco, Captain Charles E. Clark was transferred from the monitor *Monterey* and given command of the *Oregon* replacing Captain McCormick who had been ordered into the hospital. Early on the morning of March 19, 1898, the battleship, in her glistening white paint, sailed proudly out of San Francisco Bay, through the Golden Gate, on what proved to be the most renowned cruise in modern naval history.

The ship was displacing nearly 12,000 tons, but, like the officers and men, seemed to be animated with equal enthusiasm for her long 4,000 mile run to Callao, Peru, the first lap of her famous cruise. It must be recalled that the ship, when at sea, was out of communication with other ships and with the Navy Department in Washington, D. C., as radio-telegraph was not then known.

A good speed was steadily maintained for the sixteen days, although she was 27 men short in the engine crew and 67 men less than the builders furnished on her trial trip.

Ship drills began as soon as everything had been "shaken down." Ordinary peace-time routine and parades were abandoned. Morning, noon and night found the sailors at battery stations for drill and each day found the ship throwing off some outward show of peace and becoming more and more a ship being readied for war.

Soon the weather became very warm and all hands suffered the excessive heat as the ship plowed through the tropics. The men left their hammocks below and slept on deck. The thermometer ranged between 90 F. to 150 F. according to the part of the ship. What little ice the ship made was reserved for the engine room crew and firemen and coal passers. (Refrigerated, canned soft drinks had not yet been invented.)

When the equator was approached, a visit from his Gracious Majesty King Neptune, Ruler of the Seas, was received. On board were many landsmen who had never visited his domains and the day of crossing the "line" was given over to fun and frolic. All

A formal portrait of a fighting lady, the Battleship *Oregon*. But when it came time for battle, she turned out to be a snarling "bulldog."

drills were suspended in order to pay homage to the King and his Court when they came aboard. There were elaborate ceremonies that transformed the land-lubbers into Sons of the Sea. The next day discipline and drills were resumed and were not again suspended during the voyage.

Notwithstanding continuing heavy seas and head winds, the battleship continued her way operating smoothly. Regardless of the weather, the deck drills and target practice were maintained.

On the 16th day and 4,112 miles out of San Francisco, the *Oregon* anchored in the harbor of Callao where she found the gunboat *USS Marietta* (Commander Symonds), that had been sent ahead from San Francisco, with coal barges, awaiting. Here, orders were received to leave port as quickly as possible. The skipper of the battleship, with his sealed orders, had not known if he would take his warship to Manila or to Cuba.

During the coaling – 50 strenuous hours of the coal simply pouring aboard – the Chief and Assistant Engineers overhauled the engines. The hard, hot work had seen 1,100 tons placed in the bunkers plus 100 tons as deck cargo on the battleship which, added to what was left after the long run, made 1,700 tons of coal on board. During the process, the ship's steam launches patrolled around the vessels with armed guards day and night watching for any activities of the many Spaniards in the area.

Although the Peruvians were friendly, rumor came that members of the Spanish colony at Lima, 8 miles inland, had made

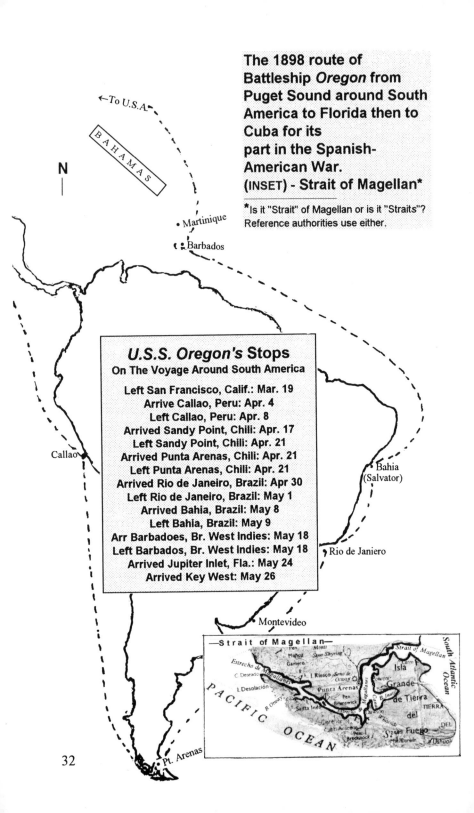

The 1898 route of Battleship *Oregon* from Puget Sound around South America to Florida then to Cuba for its part in the Spanish-American War.
(INSET) - **Strait of Magellan***

*Is it "Strait" of Magellan or is it "Straits"? Reference authorities use either.

←To U.S.A→

B A H A M A S

N

• Martinique

• Barbados

U.S.S. Oregon's Stops
On The Voyage Around South America

Left San Francisco, Calif.: Mar. 19
Arrive Callao, Peru: Apr. 4
Left Callao, Peru: Apr. 8
Arrived Sandy Point, Chili: Apr. 17
Left Sandy Point, Chili: Apr. 21
Arrived Punta Arenas, Chili: Apr. 21
Left Punta Arenas, Chili: Apr. 21
Arrived Rio de Janeiro, Brazil: Apr 30
Left Rio de Janeiro, Brazil: May 1
Arrived Bahia, Brazil: May 8
Left Bahia, Brazil: May 9
Arr Barbadoes, Br. West Indies: May 18
Left Barbados, Br. West Indies: May 18
Arrived Jupiter Inlet, Fla.: May 24
Arrived Key West: May 26

Callao

Bahia (Salvator)

Rio de Janiero

Montevideo

—Strait of Magellan—

Estrecho de Magallanes
PACIFIC OCEAN
C. Deseado
I. Desolación
Sta. Inés
Pen. Brecknock
Santa Ana
Punta Arenas
Pen. Brunswick
I. Riesco
Seno de Otway
Seno Skyring
Isla Grande de Tierra del Fuego
TIERRA
DEL
Strait of Magellan
South Atlantic Ocean
Ushuaia

Pt. Arenas

BATTLESHIP OREGON

Some researchers claim this is not *Oregon* but an artist's concept.

threats against the ship. Although no war had been declared, but not wanting to take chances, sentries and lookouts were doubled. In addition, crews for the search lights and six pounder guns were at battle stations ready for instant action. Only the Captain knew the destination of his ship.

The peace-time white paint was covered with war-time Navy gray but only on the seaward side. In harbor, during the night, the tide swung her around so by morning, the side pained gray was to seaward. The other side, with the peace-time white showing was shoreward. Curiosity seekers or spies were unaware of the trick.

Warning was received of the presence on the Atlantic coast, running out of Montevideo, of a possible interception by a Spanish torpedo-boat-destroyer, the *Temerario*. Nothing had been said as to the battleship's destination. It may have been just speculation, by newspaper editors in Peru, that the battleship could anticipate horrible things should it attempt to pass through the Straits of Magellan.

Two days at sea from Callao, the *Oregon* engineers lit the fourth boiler which brought the huge ship easily to 13 knots. This lap of the voyage, through unusually rough seas, was a distance of 2,600 miles to the Strait of Magellan.

On April 16, the *Oregon* was running before a moderate gale with thick heavy weather, trying to make the Tamar Island anchorage before dark. But the ship was unable to pass through the many reefs into the inner harbor and was obliged to anchor in fifty fathoms. Captain Clark wrote in his memoirs:

Fire in the Hold!

Some time after leaving San Francisco Bay, but before arrival in Peru, the *Oregon* was moving with a full head of steam at 12 knots generated by three or her four boilers, when it was observed that the use of fresh water was very high. Often engineers would pump in sea water for the boilers but salt water caused scale to develop with a reduction in efficiency and speed. The Chief Engineer, Robert W. Milligan, did not want to damage his recently overhauled and perfectly running ship with salt water. The Captain agreed. Even in the tropics where the seamen crave more water, the crew accepted a limit on their drinking water without open complaint. On one such hot day, a lookout spotted smoke coming up from a coal bunker. The fire-party immediately scooped out coal until the burning area, caused by spontaneous combustion, was reached and the fire put out.

Just as we entered the Straits, a violent gale struck us. The thick, hurrying scud obscured the precipitous rockbound shores and with night coming on it seemed inadvisable to proceed. With the ship driven before the gale as she was it was impossible to obtain correct soundings and making a safe anchorage must therefore be largely a matter of chance. I decided to anchor, as the lesser risk. We let go one anchor and the chain ran out furiously for about 125 fathoms before it checked. At last it caught and the other anchor was let go. They held through the night though the gale continued to rage. At early daylight we discovered that the first anchor had been dropped in 50 fathoms or, 300 feet of water. That forenoon a heavy snow storm chased us through the narrowest reaches of the Straits which in some places, is scarcely more than a mile in width.... In the afternoon we passed the wrecks of two steamers that had left their bones to mark the perils of the passage.

The spurt through the Straits of Magellan, averaging 15½ knots per hour for 11 hours, the battleship plowed through terrific storms taking much water over her bow and over her fore-13-inch turret. The effort was partially to arrive at Sandy Point (Puntas Arenas) before night but it was after dark when the ship dropped anchor there.

It was important to keep a sharp lookout for the reported Spanish warship rumored to be on the prowl for the *Oregon*. Every precaution was taken with lookouts stationed "alow and aloft" to keep strict watch for any smoke or sign of the Spaniards. But not a vessel was sighted. Nevertheless, the *Oregon* had its

The *Oregon's* two launches were coal-burning steam boats. The era was a decade before the invention of gasoline-powered outboard motors.

decks cleared for action and all hands were at battle-stations. The four searchlights were trained on the harbor in the search for the *Temerario* or any other Spanish vessel.

The people of the little town believed that war had been declared not between Spain and the United States but between Chile and Argentine and that the huge battleship was coming to bombard the town. They were very much relieved to find that it was the *U S S Oregon*. The captain of the battleship made an arrangement to rush coal on board but under the surveillance of the ship's guns and patrol boats.

On April 21st, the *Oregon* and the *Marietta* sailed out of Punta Arenas, again under sealed orders. The smaller ship steamed ahead as scout in order to signal the approach of any suspicious vessels. In the afternoon, an American steamer, bound from Montevideo to the Klondike, was spoken to by flags and the news, "prospects of peace" was received on board the battleship.

The *Oregon* was now on a war footing. No lights were shown.

The guns were kept loaded and searchlights ready for instant use. The men slept in their clothing at battle-stations on deck and in the fighting tops taking turns for resting inside the warm ship. Target practice, with all the guns of the main and secondary batteries, was held frequently. The Marietta threw barrels and boxes overboard to be targets for the gunners as the vessels steamed along.

After leaving the Straits of Magellan, the ship successfully passed through the stormy region of the heavy seas and severe gales where European pessimists had predicted disaster for the heavy battleship. Now began other dangers and long anxious days and sleepless nights for the loved ones at home.

The Marietta was making slow time and finally, the Oregon signaled her to follow into Rio de Janeiro. The battleship went ahead at fifteen knots to be able to reach Rio in the afternoon of April 30th. This would secure anchorage and get coal alongside before dark. Captain Clark recorded:

A cablegram from the Navy Department [in code] informed us that the Spanish torpedo boat Temerario was reported to have left Montevideo, probably for Rio. This was disturbing information. I got under way at once, with coal lighters alongside, and steamed up the bay nearly two miles above the man-of-war anchorage. By leaving this anchorage to the Temerario I could assume that any move she made up the bay in our direction might be certainly interpreted as hostile and would give me the right to turn our guns upon her. The Marietta, too small a pawn in the game of war, was to remain at the anchorage.

The Oregon found the cruiser Nictheroy awaiting her arrival. This ship had been purchased from Brazil, more-or-less as a way to pump a million dollars into the poor Brazilian economy, and buy some friendship. It was to join the Marietta as escort for the Oregon.

Captain Clark sent a messenger to the Brazilian Admiral that Brazil was expected to prevent any hostile acts by Spanish vessels in neutral waters. Further, the Oregon would sink any Spanish vessel that approached within half a mile of her anchorage.

The Brazilian government proved friendly and agreed to the requirements and demands. The steam cutters from the battleship patrolled at night. The searchlights played on the waters of the harbor and the guns were manned on all three American ships.

The *Marietta* was anchored as a picket vessel in such a position as to be able to cover the entrance to the harbor. At night, the Admiral sent a cruiser outside to patrol the harbor's entrance and with her searchlights, and those of the forts, it would have been impossible for a Spanish ship to enter the harbor unseen.

Everyone was starved for news. When it was announced that war had been declared, everyone cheered. The weather was very hot but the long day and night working hours, now with the enthusiasm for a shooting war about to begin for the ship, brought no complaints from the crew. Although it does not seem to be recorded, it was customary, on such occasions, for a skipper to order a light lunch be sent around to the battle-stations.

Sentries were placed on the coal barges because Spanish sympathizers with bombs in their possession had been captured near them. All of the coal was carefully inspected before it was put aboard the battleship.

On May 2, news came of the exciting action in Manila Bay by Dewey on his cruiser the *Olympia*. Immediately, the excitement turned into enthusiasm in the bay at Rio de Janeiro and the coal begrimed men fairly went wild. They danced on the coal barges and decks; then the coal came aboard faster than ever.

The officers were careful and secretive considering the dispatches received from the from the Navy Department:

Four Spanish armored cruisers, heavy and fast, sailed April 29 from Cape de Verde to the west. Destination unknown. Beware of and study carefully the situation. Must be left to your discretion entirely to avoid this fleet and to reach the United States by way of the West Indies. You can go when and where you desire. *Nictheroy* and *Marietta* subject to orders of yourself.

The Rio papers were full of Rear Admiral Pascual Cervera y Topete's fleet awaiting the *Oregon* outside the harbor. The Brazilian Admiral sent a cruiser to prevent any engagement in neutral waters.

Captain Clark's answer to the Department was:

The receipt of telegram of May 3 is acknowledged. Will proceed in obedience to orders I have received. Keeping near the Brazilian coast, as the Navy Department considers the Spanish fleet from Cape de Verde superior, will be unsuitable. I can coal from the *Nictheroy*, if necessity compels it, to reach the United States. If the *Nictheroy* delays too much I shall hasten passage leaving her with the *Marietta*. Every department of the *Oregon* in fine condition.

The following day the Captain called all hands to the quarter deck and read the portion of the dispatches which told that the Spanish fleet was supposed to be in search of the battleship. The crew of 500 men promptly joined in cheers for the *Oregon*. The ship was already cleared for action and every preparation was made to meet the enemy's fleet. Even the mahogany pilot house was dismantled to a skeleton in order to prevent its being set on fire by a Spanish shell. The ship had been painted a dull gray war color, now nearly a century later affectionately called "battleship-gray." This American battleship was ready for war.

"Providential Good Fortune"

The fact that the *Oregon* did not encounter the Spanish fleet near Cape St. Roque "was a piece of providential good fortune wholly on the side of the Spanish commander" wrote Edward S. Ellis (see bibliography). As later events established, had the Spanish fleet and the *Oregon* met in an unscheduled rendezvous in mid-ocean, because the *Oregon* had heavier guns and better gunners, and not all the enemy's guns would work, conceivably *Oregon* could have shot all of the Spanish ships out of the ocean before any of them reached Cuba.

Before leaving Rio, the boys purchased a large supply of red ribbon which was made into cap bands for the crew and arm bands for the officers bearing stenciled letters:

REMEMBER THE MAINE

The arm of every officer and the cap of every crewman bore this legend throughout the war.

After dark, on May 8, the *Oregon* anchored in the harbor of Bahia (Salvator), Brazil for a day's delay and to send a coded cablegram to Washington:

Much delayed by the *Marietta* and *Nictheroy*. Left them near Cape Frio with orders to come on or beach if necessary to avoid capture. The *Oregon* could steam fourteen knots for hours, and in running fight, might beat off and even cripple the Spanish fleet. With present amount of coal on board will be in good fighting trim and could reach West Indies. If more should be taken here I could reach Key West; but in that case belt-armor, cellulose belt and protective deck would be below water line. Whereabouts of Spanish fleet requested.

In the evening the answer came:

> Proceed at once to Key West without further stop in Brazil. No authentic news of the Spanish fleet. Avoid if possible. We believe that you will defeat it if met.

During the night of May 9, the *Oregon* again went to sea standing well-off the coast in order to make a wide sweep around Cape St. Roque, where Admiral Cervera's fleet was again reported to be waiting. It will be recalled that the battleship was always operating under secret orders thus it seems unlikely, in these days before radio, that the Spanish knew where she was.

In the event of a meeting with the Spanish ships, Captain Clark's plan was to proceed at full speed under forced draft and head away from the enemy. Such a tactic was to "string out" the Spanish vessels in their chase. When the enemy's leading ship should approach within range, the *Oregon* was to turn on her and attack, then devote attention to the other slower ships that were following. *

Only two of the Spanish warships were rated to be as fast as the *Oregon* and by making a running fight, it was fully expected that the battleship would eliminate the possibility of being surrounded and rammed or torpedoed.

On the evening of May 12, a number of lights were sighted which had the appearance of a fleet sailing in double column. Not a light was showing on the *Oregon* and she passed through the midst of "lights" undetected, for she could not have been seen a hundred yards ahead. What these lights were was never positively determined but, according to the log of the *Cristobal Colon,* the Spanish squadron was off Cape St. Roque at that time.

On May 15, the *Oregon* made a run of 375 miles and on the 18th, anchored in the harbor of Bridgetown, Barbados. Her majesty's officials were friendly and gave the *Oregon* a cordial welcome, but rigidly enforced neutrality laws.

There, rumors reached Captain Clark that the Spanish fleet was at Martinque just 90 miles away and that the enemy's vessels were seen cruising off the Barbadoes the day before. With the

---

* How well this theory would have succeeded was clearly established on July 3rd when this maneuver was, by chance, executed but in this instance, it was the *Oregon* doing the chase and overtook each of the slower Spanish vessels instead of their chasing the *Oregon.*

enemy's vessels reported to be all around her, the *Oregon* hurriedly coaled and stole out of the harbor that night after announcing the intention to leave the next morning.

With all lights burning brightly, she set a direct course to Key West. After sailing only five miles, all lights were extinguished and the *Oregon* turned about. The ship made a sweep around Barbados then laid a course well to the eastward of all the islands. This maneuver frustrated any night attack should news have been sent to Martinique of the *Oregon's* whereabouts.

The battleship passed to the north of the Bahamas and after dark, on May 24th, the American shore was sighted. Shortly, the great ship dropped anchors off Jupiter Inlet, Florida. A boat was sent ashore to communicate with Washington:

Oregon arrived. Have coal enough to reach Dry Tortugas or Hampton Roads. Boat landing through surf awaits orders.

About two in the morning the answer came:

If ship is in good condition and ready for service, go to Key West, otherwise to Hampton Roads. The Department congratulates you upon your safe arrival which has been announced to the President.

The anchors were hove up in a hurry and light and happy were the hearts that were soon on their way to Key West. There, they joined Admiral Sampson's fleet then in Cuban waters. The *Oregon* arrived at Key West May 26 where 500 tons of coal were taken aboard. Here the men received the first letters and papers and learned that the eyes of the world had been on the *Oregon* for many weeks and that much speculation and many rumors had been telegraphed to the ends of the earth regarding the unheard of long voyage of a battleship.

Captain Clark received congratulatory messages from many parts of the country. This telegram came from the Navy:

The Department congratulates you, your officers and crew upon the completion of your long remarkably successful voyage.

All hands were called to muster on the evening of the 26th of May when Captain Clark read the congratulatory telegram from the Secretary of the Navy. Almost immediately the *Wilmington* crossed the bow of the battleship and gave her the first of many "Three cheers for the *Oregon*"!

After such a long voyage any large vessel should be in need of cleaning, oiling, adjusting of its working parts. Several weeks time would seem excessive to spend in such rehabilitation. Once at anchor and the engines cooled, after completing a few adjustments to its machinery, the *Oregon* was ready to fire-up and move out at 1:04 a.m. on May 29th. It had been less than three days since her arrival, she steamed away from Key West to add her strength to that of the Atlantic fleet off the coast of Cuba.

When the *Oregon* came within sight of the flagship, the *Brooklyn*, the admiral ran up signal flags reading:

Put into port for over hauling.

Captain Clark replied:

We are ready to fight.

The O*regon* was received with many cheers and shouts of approval from the other ships and the band on the *Indiana* played the new popular tune: "New Bully."

On the morning of May 30, in company with the flag ship, the *USS Oregon* steamed to Santiago and reached there the morning of June 1. Here again she was hailed with cheers and congratulations from all the ships of the blockading squadron.

Then came long weary nights and long days of waiting for the enemy, which had bottled up itself in Santiago's Harbor, to either come out and fight or run up the white flag of surrender.

Little incidents came up every day to vary the monotony of being on lookout for enemy activity.

Admiral Schley, second in command of the American fleet (in the *U.S.S. Brooklyn* - above) ordered the U. S. Navy to close for battle.

On June 2nd, the *Oregon* was detailed to duty as guard ship. A boat was sighted and the battleship was signaled to give chase. After a long run under forced draft, it was found to be a newspaper reporter's boat making for the mole St. Nicholas, with all possible speed, to send news to the United States. Captain Clark told this story many times and added the saying of some wag on board another ship:

There goes Clark off for the Pacific again. Things are too slow for him here. Good-bye.

On the afternoon of June 3d, the *Oregon* and the *Texas* were ordered to approach the harbor with a cable boat between them to cut the telegraph cable. When near the entrance, they were surprised to see a tug boat coming out of the harbor flying a white flag. All the men of the American fleet were utterly disgusted thinking the whole Spanish fleet was surrendering. But that was not the reason for the flag. The tug brought news of the brave Hobson and his eight men who, the night before, had sunk the *Merrimak* in the channel of the harbor making it difficult for not more than one boat at a time to enter or leave the harbor.

A strict blockade was held, at all times, around the harbor's mouth in the form of a semi-circle. Early one morning the *St. Paul* came in with a collier flying a British flag under guard. The steamer was taken as countraband of war for trying to smuggle coal to the Spanish fleet.

On the night of June 4th, at about 10:30 p.m., there was a call to general quarters. Guns promptly opened fire opened on a torpedo boat-destroyer that had ventured out of the harbor. The next morning two torpedoes were found floating in the harbor but the torpedo boat was either sunk in the dark or escaped into one of the many inlets along the coast.

On the morning of June 6th, the bugle sounded:

CLEAR SHIP FOR ACTION

Slowly the American ships steamed within range of the forts and opened a fierce cannonade. These gunners in the forts return-ed the fire. After a short span of time, battery after battery on the island was silenced by the American gunners. On the night of June 11, *Oregon* took her turn at keeping the searchlights of the vessel playing on the harbor entrance. This practice was kept up

Beam from carbon-arc searchlights cut the sky and were effective for several miles. See the picture on page 99.

until after the shout between the ships and the forts for the powerful rays of the carbon arc lights made it nearly impossible for the any ship to leave the harbor without the American squadron seeing the movement.

Again, on the 16th, the sailors were called to general quarters and the ship cleared for action to fire on the forts. Marine Private Robert Cross, on the *Oregon*, wrote in his diary:

> *June 16*: At 3:30 A.M. this morning all hands were called to coffie and hard tack and cand Beef at 4 A.M. Some 15 or 20 minutes later Gen Quarters sounded. Then we went and try to knock out those Batterys off the earth. Bombarded until 7:15 A.M. Nobody knows

how much damage was don, except, we silenced all the Batterys they had.

The results were the same: No casualties but great damage done to the shore batteries.

On June 17, the *Oregon* was ordered to Guantanamo where 300 tons of coal were taken aboard. After casting loose from the colliers, the big guns of the ship were trained upon the town of Caimaners. This was at a distance of 7,500 yards. Several shells landed in the town doing some damage and caused the frightened inhabitants to leave with haste.

June 26th saw more shelling by the *Oregon* and the other ships all shooting at Morro Castle. The *Oregon* eventually went to within 700 yards of a shore battery and with an 8-inch shell, knocked down the Spanish flag – also knocked over one of the shore guns. Cross opined:

> I believe if the flag ship had not signaled us off, Capt. Clark would have went in along side of old Morro and give him a tutching up.

From this time until July 3, the routine of blockade duty was continued. The searchlights played their eerie columns of blue-white "daylight" on the harbor every night while the steam cutters from the ships patrolling the anchored American ships to guard against small boats sneaking through.

The night of July 2, the *Oregon* had been ordered to return to Guantanamo Bay for coaling. A spy at the fort intercepted the message and the Spanish fleet, assuming that the *Oregon* would not be in the blockade the next morning, decided to try to a get away. From the very first, the Spaniards had been afraid to face the *Oregon's* awesome firepower. But *Oregon's* order had been canceled so she stayed in the blockade line and a different ship sent for coal.

The flagship *New York*, with Admiral William T. Sampson aboard, was at Alteras, seven miles from the harbor's entrance, and was just getting under way to go to Siboney where the Admiral intended on conferring with General Shafter. This conference was to consider the advisability of making a joint attack upon the enemy's defense afloat and ashore when the naval battle began on the 3rd. He ordered his ship to return to the blockade

line and rushed there with all speed only to arrive for the culmination of the fight.*✛

**Battleship *Oregon*. Location unknown. The mast
was for hoisting signal flags. There were no radios.**

---

* Controversy was caused when the newspapers credited Admiral Winfield Scott Schley (sl-
eye) with the victory because at the beginning of the engagement, Admiral Sampson was, as
we have seen, several miles away but Schley's cruiser, the *Brooklyn* was a part of the
running battle. Admiral Schley was second in command of the naval force, under Admiral
Sampson, blockading Santiago de Cuba. As Admiral Sampson was not immediately on the
scene when the battle began, Adm. Schley directed the action and became the central figure
in the unfortunate controversy over to whom should be credited for the American victory.

45

Tail stingers – 13" guns of the *Oregon*.

3. Historic Battle of Santiago de Cuba

Sunday morning, July 3, dawned clear, bright and warm. The waters around the war ships was as calm as a lake. There was no wind. Decks had just been scrubbed and the battleship *Oregon* was spic-and-span. Officers and men had changed into their whites and every one was ready for muster for general inspection. The sailors would listen to a reading of the *Articles of War* by an officer. This document detailed the rules of conduct and punishments to be meted out for infractions. Both the Army and the Navy believed that the regularly reading of this very lengthy epistle would keep the men in line. It was a standing order in the Navy for the men to hear the *Articles of War* on the first Sunday of every month.

Joseph C. Gannon served as a signalman on the *Oregon* during the action. His duty was to be "top side" and instantly ready to hoist or lower signal flags on the order of the ship's commander or the duty officer. On the 3rd of July he was in the chart house. When he glanced toward the shore he though he saw columns of black smoke near the harbor's mouth. He mentioned this scene to the man at the ship's wheel who acknowledged it was smoke. The helmsman said the Chief Quartermaster determined it was the Spanish ships trying to sneak out of the harbor, then the Chief had left for the conning tower.

Gannon later wrote that in looking at the sight through a spy glass, he saw the bow of a ship emerging at fairly high speed. Then he saw three more ships following closely all with battle flags flying and shooting at anything the gunners viewed. Both he and the quartermaster reached for the switch for the alarm but Gannon reached it first noticing the chart house clock at 9:28.

As the general alarm ("battle-stations") broke the stillness of placid morning air, men on the deck yelled, tore off dress shirts,

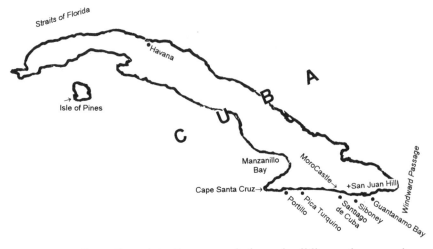

caps – flung them into the sea and cheered wildly as they raced for their guns. Cross's diary reveals:

> All of a sudden the Ordly on watch made a dive for the Cabin head first, and told the old man the Fleet was coming out of Harbor. the old man jumpt up standing. as soon as some men seen the ships, they went to there Quarters without any dealy. I was standing on the Quarter Deck waiting for the last call to go when I heard the news and lookng around the affter Terets seen the first ship. I thought it looked Biger than a Mountain But then I thought we could cut her down to natcheral size of course it takes longer to tell about it than it taken us to get ready, for we wer allways ready and all we had to do was sound the Bells and stand By our Guns, they wer allways loaded so all we had to do was to turn on the fors draught and pull the trigger.

Only seconds later, the roar of a shot from one of the battle-ship's 6-pounder guns, fired by a Marine (Private Joseph H. O'Shay), split the air. Immediately the gunner shouted to the bridge that the range on his trial shot was 3,200 yards. The shell splashed between two of the enemy warships. Shay's shell, fired at 9:29 a.m., from the *USS Oregon,* was the first shot from the United States Navy in the Battle of Santiago de Cuba.

Without warning, the Spanish fleet was making a run for the open sea. The *Maria Teresa* turned toward the west. In her wake were the *Viscaya* then the *Cristobal Colon* followed by the *Oquendo* and two torpedo boat-destroyers, the *Pluton* and the *Furor.* For thirty-four days the American squadron had watched the "Hole in the Wall" praying for the fleet to come out of the harbor, where it had been bottled up, and give battle.Here they were at last.

Cheers rang from vessel to vessel while shouts of "There they are, there they are," filled the air. Led by the *Infanta Maria Teresa,* one of the most powerful warships of the world of that day, the Spanish fleet swept majestically out through the narrow channel from the harbor of Santiago. Large red and yellow ensigns stood out brilliantly against the dark background of Morro Castle and the headlands. The ships' massive black hulls, with great white waves piled under their bows, seemed veritable things of life.

Who Was in Command?

Admiral Sampson's flagship, the battleship *New York*, was not part of the American blockade line as Spanish Admiral Cervera's fleet rushed out of the harbor for Sampson was away on other business. Commodore Schley, the second in command on *Brooklyn*, hoisted his flag now as acting commander and ordered the Atlantic Squadron to close in for battle.

The *Oregon* had been kept in readiness, by Chief Engineer Milligan, to go into battle at a moment's notice consequently, had steam up to give the vessel an almost immediate ten knots while the other ships started the chase with only five or six knots speed.

The OREGON charged ahead passing the *Texas* on her port side at a distance that in peacetime would have been considered too close for comfort. Out of the smoke of gunnery, the *Iowa* suddenly appeared at 9:50 a.m. so close that the Oregon put the helm hard-over to avoid collision then the *Brooklyn* crossed the bows of *Texas* and *Oregon*, all this melee* in the effort to get underway to sink the Spanish ships.

The *Oregon* plowed ahead in her quest. She first took on the *Maria Teresa* that was in serious trouble, and afire, having been raked with heavy shells from the *Indiana* and the *Iowa*. At about 800 yards, Captain Clark ordered a hellish fire at the ship causing

---

* Joe Gannon wrote: "I figured [with] a good long toss, I could have landed a potato on the deck of the *Iowa*."

the *Infanta Maria Teresa* to pile itself on the rocks only six miles from Santiago. This Spanish armored cruiser was out of the war.

The *Oregon* now charged after the *Almirante Oquendo*. At about 900 yards, the *Oregon* let loose with its heavy, medium and smaller guns resulting in a serious, uncontrollable fire forward on the Spaniard. The flames stretched back for the bridge and the mast-top. Even so, the *Oquendo's* gunners returned the fire to the extent possible. Finally, with the range between the ships continuing to reduce, very shortly the *Oquendo,* foundering, turned toward the shore and piled up in a mass of flames a short half-mile from the *Maria Teresa.* (The destroyer *Pluton* had also been sunk here.)

The cruiser *Oquendo*: wrecked, beached, abandoned. On guns, note breechlocks are missing. Did the Spanish go to war with non-firable guns?　　——Photos by Wm. R. Hearst.

Oil painting of a scene during height of the Battle of Santiago.

At this point, Captain Clark directed that the hard-working men below decks be allowed to come up a few at a time, get a breath of fresh air and look at the burning and beached *Oquendo.* With enthusiasm anew, the black-gang worked harder than ever sending the *Oregon* ahead at highest speed.

> The *Oregon's* hot pursuit [in the Spanish-American War] was the moon landing of its day. —Ted Mahar, The *Oregonian*

Commodore Schley, on *Brooklyn,* signaled the *Oregon* to "close up" therefore the battleship closed on the *Viscaya* firing from 3,000 yards, but kept an eye on the *Cristobal Colon* to the west. The *Oregon* kept firing at the *Viscaya* down to 900 yards. The time was 10:22. The Spanish ship appeared as if he might ram the American ship, by heading right for it, but ended the run placing herself directly across the *Oregon's* bow – not a wise place to be!

The *Viscaya* was faced with a dilemma. The *Oregon* was on her starboard bow and the *Brooklyn,* which was approximately parallel, on the left, with the *Oregon.* The *Viscaya* took on the *Brooklyn* with her forward guns and shot at the *Oregon* with port side guns. At this time, a tremendous shell exploded on the Spanish warship's port bow, probably from the *Oregon,* while a second shell exploded amid-ships.

Heavily aflame, the *Viscaya* turned for the beach where it too piled up near the town of Accadorus, eighteen miles from the harbor where she had been safe for weeks.

Remains of *Infanta Maria Teresa* after being fired by shells from *Indiana* and *Iowa*, then, hellish fire from *Oregon's* big guns forced the Spanish cruiser to pile up on the rocks only 6 miles from Santiago. —Photo by Wm. R. Hearst

A limited supply of Cardiff coal was taken aboard while at Mare Island Ship Yard northeast of San Francisco. This hard coal put out a very hot fire. To make certain it was not mixed with the bituminous and its special worth lost, Chief Engineer R. W. Milligan kept the Cardiff bunker locked to save that coal when it might be especially needed. On July 3rd, during the running battle to catch the *Cristobal Colon*, he opened the bunker and ordered the coal passers to use this prized fuel.

Commodore Schley on *Brooklyn,* sent flags aloft reading:

OREGON – WELL DONE

Then began a chase after the *Cristobal Colon*. This was the sole Spanish ship remaining that had escaped from the harbor,

The *Brooklyn* and the *Oregon* now turned their attention to the *Cristobal Colon*, the latter being fully six miles away and running at its best speed.

We hark back to one of the coaling stops where the Chief Engineer was able to obtain a limited tonnage of Cardiff coal. This is a hard coal putting out a much hotter fire than the bituminous coal commonly used by the U. S. Navy. He was so pleased to have it that he is reported to have stored it in locked bin against a time when truly maximum performance would be needed. Was this the time?

52

Captain Charles E. Clark, USN,
Commander of Battleship *Oregon*
at Battle of Santiago de Cuba.
(Right) Wm. Randolph Hearst
making pictures during the battle.

> As the *Colon* made her gallant dash for liberty,
> Clark of the *Oregon* saw his job clearly cut out for
> him and without an instant's hesitation, but his helm
> to star-board and came through the lee of the *Iowa*
> with the speed of a locomotive. Captain Evans, *USS IOWA*

With the Spanish ship miles ahead, and the *Oregon* running at top speed, the battleship needed an extra *oomph* if it were to overhaul the *Cristobal Colon*. Engineer Milligan unlocked his Cardiff coal and ordered the black-gang to shovel it fast and furiously into the fire boxes. It seemed only seconds before the great battle wagon took on a burst of speed and passed the *Brooklyn*. The battleship, rated at 15-knots, moved out at 16-knots without hesitation and held this for about three hours until the *Cristobal Colon* was inside gunnery range. This, after the arduous rounding of South America and no formal overhaul.

A well-placed 13-inch shell hit the *Cristobal Colon* under its stern then the next shot went over the ship splashing into the water before its bow. With his ship bracketed, the Spanish captain knew his flight was over for if he continued to run, the *Oregon* would sink him. He promptly dropped his colors. Seeing this, *Oregon* stopped shooting.

The *Brooklyn* sent a dispatch boat, under the cover of the *Oregon's* guns to the Spaniard to accept the surrender.

The Spanish armored cruiser quit the battle at 1:12 p.m. only 51 miles out of Santiago.

The thundering of the *Oregon's* heavy guns was replaced by the strains of first, "There 'll Be A Hot Time In The Old Town Tonight" then followed "The Star Spangled Banner" played by the *Oregon's* band which had assembled on deck. Also on decks and in rigging were most of the battleship's 504 officers, sailors and marines many bare to the waist and begrimed with powder smoke and coal dust. They were embracing one another, dancing around and cheering with that fervor and joy which mark the overflowing of hearts of men who know they had been looking into the face of death but escaped victoriously. There were rousing cheers for the Captain followed by the tender words he spoke to the crew. The *Brooklyn* hoisted signal flags reading:

CONGRATULATIONS UPON YOUR GLORIOUS VICTORY

A prize crew from the *Oregon* was sent to board the *Cristobal Colon*. Alas: Just before the surrender, the Spanish had opened and damaged the valves and stop-cocks. The ship was filling with water. Despite the efforts of the prize crew, the *Cristobal Colon* sank.

Captain Evans of the *Iowa* said:

Captain Clark of the *Oregon* saw his job and without an instant's hesitation came through with the speed of as locomotive. We may all live a hundred years and fight fifty naval battles but we can never hope to see such a sight as the *Oregon* was on this beautiful Sunday morning.

—(Century Magazine May 1899 pp 54-55.)

The next morning, July 4, American Independence Day, the

The Stars and Stripes Forever
March
JOHN PHILIP SOUSA

This was 1898. John Philip Sousa, the March King, was a very patriotic man and had been the Conductor of the Marine Band. In 1896 he wrote a new march which was immediately adopted by bandmasters. While there does not seem to be documentation for which of the many Sousa marches the *Oregon's* band played after the naval battle of 1898, there is every reason to believe the new "The Stars and Striped Forever" was included. Few people today realize there are words to it:

Let martial note in triumph float and liberty extend its mighty hand,
  A flag appears mid thund'rous cheers, the banner of the Western land.
The emblem of the brave and true, its folds protect no tyrant crew,
  The red and white and starry blue, is freedom's shield and hope.
Other nations may deem their flags the best and cheer them with fervid elation,
  But the flag of the North and South and West is the flag of flags,
The flag of freedom's nation.

Chorus:

Hurrah for the flag of the free, May it wave as our standard for ever,
  The gem of the land and the sea, The banner of the right.
Let despots remember the day when our fathers with mighty endeavor
  Proclaimed as they marched to the fray,
That by their might and by their right, it waves forever.

—Copyright: MDCCCXCIX by The John Church Company

55

The grand parade of the Atlantic Fleet, led by the *U.S.S. Oregon*, (*U.S.S. Texas* behind and to left) in the Hudson River following the battle surrounded by hundreds of harbor craft.

U.S.S. Oregon (stern view) on parade in the Hudson River.

conquering battleship *Oregon* sailed back over the route of the victory of the day before and witnessed the sad results of war. It saw the pride, the power, and the glory of Spain piled up in burning wrecks or partly sunk below the water for miles along the Cuban coast.

The *Oregon's* 4th of July reception by the fleet off Santiago and Commodore Schley's signal

WELCOME BACK BRAVE OREGON

was an occasion to remember for a lifetime. It was a glorious 4th of July.

Captain Clark had undergone a long and continuous strain both mentally and physically during the months since leaving the Pacific coast. When the battle was over, the pent-up strain proved too much for him so he received orders for hospitalization. He had endeared himself to his officers and men. On August 6th, he left the ship and was rowed from the *Oregon* by officers, the highest compliment paid to a commander when leaving his ship.

On August 7th, Capt. A. S. Barker, who had commanded the battleship *Oregon* earlier, was ordered to again take the ship.*

On August 14, the flagships *Brooklyn* and *New York* along with the battleships *Iowa, Massachusetts, Indiana* and *Oregon* weighed anchor and started for the Hudson River. All of New

---

*The *Oregon* was assigned to the Atlantic Eastern Raiding Squadron and it became the flagship. The squadron, made up of the *Oregon, Massachusetts* and *New York*, with attendant smaller vessels, was to hunt for a Spanish battleship near the European coast. The flotilla did not sail because of the destruction of the Spanish fleet at Santiago.

York was to turn out in gala attire to welcome the six most formidable warships in the in the world – especially the *Oregon* the "bull dog" of them all.

*   *   *

Publisher William Randolph Hearst was still promoting his New York *Evening Journal* and he, as well as everyone else in the great city, knew that the fleet would cruise up the Hudson on August 20th. While the city waited in anticipation of the naval parade, Hearst was busy. He would manipulate the city's celebration to give the impressions it was a Hearst newspaper-sponsored holiday and the Navy was on hand at the invitation of Hearst!

In his paper for August 21st, he urged the mayor to proclaim a city-wide holiday thereby closing business so everyone could turn out for the parade. The mayor didn't go for the ruse replying he didn't have authority to declare a holiday. But he did encourage businessmen to "give up business as fully as possible" so the day would be holiday-like.

Hearst proclaimed that the *Journal's* dispatch boat, *Anita,* that had operated in Cuban waters, would lead the battleships up

---

American Casualties

In the Spanish War in 114 days of action, the U. S. Navy suffered 1 officer and 17 men killed. For the Army, 29 officers and 440 men killed. The Navy's good health saw only 56 deaths from disease of an average strength of 26,102. To disease the Army lost 676 officers and 1,872 men of an average strength of 227,494.

---

the river. Of course, the gallant *Oregon* would be part of this parade and it was the *Oregon* people wanted to cheer.

On Saturday, August 14, when Admiral Sampson's fleet headed up the Hudson River, the water was loaded with some 400 vessels. There was everything from tugboats, fishing boats, ocean liners, ferry boats, yachts all blowing steam whistles. Even men in row boats stood and waved their 10¢ flags. Shore batteries fired thunderous salutes and the salutes were returned by guns of the fleet and lo! There was the little *Anita,* sporting huge banners, promoting the *Journal* out in front. This was an example of Publisher Hearst running with the bit in his teeth on his often preposterous promotions just to sell his newspapers.

The other publishers in town took a dim-view of Hearst's doings but were used to this as well as being powerless to curb him. Nevertheless, the hundreds of thousands of people who assembled along the river to cheer the fleet that day was never surpassed until throngs turned out in even greater numbers decades later. These events were for the parade of tall ships during the Bicentennial celebration of the United States of America (July 4, 1976) and for the centennial and rededication of the Statue of Liberty *(July 3 - 6, 1986). ✛

SCUTTLED
A prize crew from the *Oregon*, commanded by the battleship's Executive Officer Lt. Cdr. James K. Cogswell, climbed aboard the *Cristobal Colon*. The plan was to inspect and determine salvage possibilities when it was discovered that the sea-cocks had been pulled and the ship was on the verge of sinking. The American crew abandoned the hulk about 11 a.m. only minutes before the wreck rolled onto its side.

What if?

As the *Oregon* approached Barbados, because there was no radio, neither the U. S. Navy headquarters nor the Spanish headquarters knew where their ships were even though Captain Clark had traded cablegrams with Washington back at Rio. While Washington worriers wondered of the risk of a possible contact at sea, and how their lone battleship would survive against Spain's 4 armored cruisers and 3 destroyers, as was later determined, the Spanish believed the *Oregon* was still in the Pacific Ocean. But Clark was not napping. He had envisioned a running battle if he encountered the Spanish. In looking at the specifications of the Spanish ships, although technically rated on paper as faster, he was convinced not one of Admiral Cevera's cruisers could have caught the *Oregon* had the battleship decided to run. If a fight started, because of the battleship's bigger guns, expertly trained officers and crew and a spirit to win, there seems little doubt that the *Oregon* would have sunk every Spanish ship. If so, the history of the Spanish-American War would have been altered for their would have been no Battle of Santiago.

Doomed From the Start?
Before he left Spain, Adm Cervera complained to Spanish authorities that the mission to Cuba was ill advised due to "insufficient coal, provisions and ammunition and that some of the ships even lacked their guns." —*The Oxford Companion to Ships & the Sea*

Principal American Naval Commanders
Spanish-American War

Admiral William Thomas Sampson. 1840-1902. American naval officer graduated from U. S. Naval Academy Annapolis 1861. _Importance here_: Commander in chief North Atlantic Squadron in Spanish-American War. Earlier: Served in Civil War. President, Board of Inquiry into destruction of battleship _Maine_ (Havana, Cuba 1898); In Spanish-American War the fleet under his command destroyed Spanish fleet under Cervera when it attempted to escape from Bay at Santiago de Cuba (July 3, 1898). When the U.S.. press credited victory to Adm. Schley, controversy occurred due to Adm. Sampson's being a few miles away to attend conference with General Shafter at the moment of start of battle and Schley's cruiser _Brooklyn_ was present and took active part in the running battle. Rear Admiral (1899). Remembered on U.S. postage stamp (1937).

Admiral Winfield Scott Schley. (pron: sly) USN. 1839-1911. American naval officer graduated U.S. Naval Academy Annapolis 1860. _Importance here_: Second to Admiral Sampson in commanding naval force in blockade of Santiago de Cuba (1898). Earlier: Commanded rescue mission in Arctic (1884) searching for Lt. Adolphius W. Greely. In the Spanish-American War because of absence of Adm. Sampson when naval engagement with Spanish began, assumed command and directed action that resulted in destruction of Spanish fleet (July 3, 1898). Unfortunate center of controversy over assignment for credit for American victory. Rear Admiral (1899). Retired 1901. Remembered on U.S. postage stamp (1937).

Admiral George Dewey. 1837-1917. American Naval officer graduated U.S. Naval Academy, Annapolis 1858. _Importance here_: He destroyed Spanish Asiatic fleet in Battle of Manila Bay (May 1, 1898). Earlier: In Civil War served under Farragut. Commanding officer U.S. Asiatic Squadron (Jan 3, 1898); took squadron to Hong Kong where on Apr. 20 he learned of declaration of war with Spain. Hong Kong invited him to leave which he did sailing for Manila where he attacked Spanish naval squadron and won Supported Army in capture of Manila (Aug. 13). Admiral USN from 1899. President, general board U.S. Navy Dept., Wash. D.C. 1900-1917. Remembered on U.S. postage stamp (1937).

Principal Spanish Naval Commander
Spanish-American War

Admiral Pascual Cerve´ra y Tope´te. Conde de Jerez´. Marqués de San´ta A´na. 1839-1909. Spanish Naval Academy of San Fernando (1848-1851). *Importance here*: Commander of Spanish squadron in Spanish-American War (1898). Earlier: Naval officer in Morocco (1859); Philippines, Cuba (1868-1878) and other station assignments. Minister of Marine, admiral, adjutant to queen regent; head of Spanish commission to London Naval Conference (1891). In his attempt to break the American blockade of harbor of Santiago de Cuba (July 3, 1898) he was defeated; became prisoner of war. Returned to Spain (Sept. 1898). Became Vice admiral (1901). Chief of staff, Spanish Navy (1902). Senator (1903).

This Is How It Was

A paragraph taken from a letter written by Sergeant of Marines Fred A. Ramsey to his father in McMinnville, Oregon:

We were waiting for assembly on July 3, when the Chief Quartermaster reported: 'The enemy's ships are coming out of the harbor, Sir.' In an instant all the long glasses on the bridge were directed toward the harbor. Lieut. Wm. H. Allen was officer of the deck. We could see him smile and take a good look with his glasses in order to be sure before he sent word to the Captain. He coolly lowered his glasses and telephoned to the orderly: 'Tell the Captain that the enemy's ships are steaming out of the harbor.' As soon as the word was repeated to Captain Clark, he touched the electric button starting the signal gongs ringing throughout the ship that notified every man to get to his station for battle quickly. I will never forget the grand sight we witnessed on that morning – four first class cruisers, two torpedo boats and one torpedo boat destroyer, steaming out of the harbor one after the other at full speed. The *Oregon* was a little over 3 miles off the entrance of the harbor when we first sighted them and we sounded our whistle three times, then Private O'Shea fired the challenging shot from a six-pounder as the first ship's bow came into view around Morro Castle. This shot was followed by an 8-inch armor piercing shell from our after 8-inch turret on the starboard side. The *Oregon* was the first to see the enemy, the first to fire a shot and the last to fire a shot at the close of the action.

Retaliation

About 1:15 p.m., July 3, 1898, when the *Oregon* and *Brooklyn* were chasing the *Cristobal Colon*, and the *Colon,* shelled by the *Oregon* had just surrendered, the *Oregon* raised the signal flags reading: REMEMBER THE MAINE
The *Brooklyn* answered: WE DID

The Battle of Santiago
"The Naval Battle of the Ages"
July 3, 1898

Spanish ships sighted at 9:28 a.m.

USS Oregon (battleship) fired first shot: 9:29 a.m.

Pluton (destroyer - torpedo boat) shelled, sank 4 miles from harbor.

Furor (destroyer - torpedo boat) shelled, sank 4 miles from harbor.

Maria Teresa (cruiser - flagship) afire, crashed on rocks 6 miles from harbor at ±10:10 a.m.

Almirante Oquindo (cruiser) afire, beached less than 1/2 mile from flagship at ±10:20 a.m.

Viscaya (cruiser) afire, beached 18 miles from harbor ±11:00 a.m. .

USS Oregon hits *Cristobal Colon* (cruiser) with 13-inch shell at 1:12 p.m. *Colon* surrendered at sea, about 51 miles from harbor, is scuttled by Spanish crew.

The Naval Battle of the Spanish-American War was over after 3 hours and 43 minutes.

The *USS Oregon*, "Bulldog of the Navy," fired the first and last shots of the battle.

4. Return to the Pacific

After anchoring in the Hudson River for a week to let the public view the famous battleship *Oregon*, the ship pulled anchors and cruised down stream to the Brooklyn Navy Yard. It had been more than one year since the last formal inspection, clean, oil and adjust.

The ship had been in the cool waters of the North Pacific Ocean, (49° N) cruised through the tropics to the Straits of Magellan (53° S) then north as far as New York (40° N) picking up tons of barnacles and seaweed on her bottom along the way. Some writers about naval affairs shake their heads in wonder that the ship performed so well while carrying 1) an overload of coal, 2) a heavily encrusted bottom load of sea-debris. Despite all this extra load, the *Oregon* had out-run all the other vessels of the American and Spanish fleets.

In the shipyard, now that the war was presumably over, the battleship was once again painted white. Visitors by the thousands flocked to the visit the ship.

While at sea, many of the sailor's* terms of enlistment's had run out. These men were discharged. Others were transferred to other duty at the convenience of the Navy. Some men sought transfers to other ships and there were many elsewhere in the navy who wanted duty on the battleship *Oregon*.

On completing the tour in the navy yard, the *Oregon* was ordered to join the fleet of Admiral George Dewey in Manila Bay. The battleship was to be the command ship for this service squadron:

Oregon,	battleship
Iowa,	battleship
Celtic,	refrigerated stores ship –ice-maker
Scindia,	collier

---

* For rosters of officers and men on the ship during the Battle of Santiago de Cuba, see Appendices A, B, C, D.

The ships departed on October 12, 1898 setting course along the coast of South America. There was no rush. This was a leisurely "show-the flag" voyage. At Bahia, they were joined by the *Iris,* * a fresh-water distillery ship and the *Justin,* a collier, then put in at Rio de Janeiro on November 11th. At Rio, the ships helped the country celebrate the anniversary of the Brazilian Republic on November 12. There were several public entertainments for the visitors including a visit to the *Oregon* by the retiring president of Brazil. On the 15th, captains and other officers of the flotilla, officially attended the inauguration of the new president. On the evening of the 16th, a formal reception was held aboard the *Oregon* at which over one thousand prominent people of Brazil were guests.

On the 18th, the new president reviewed the squadron then visited aboard the *Oregon* taking the opportunity to thank the United States for its interests in his country. On the next day, the flotilla departed for Uruguay.

After being entertained at Montevideo, the ships left for the Straits of Magellan and a stop at Punta Arenas where they arrived on December 7th. The trip through the Straits was considerably more relaxed this time compared with the earlier eastward run under forced draft to get to the blockade of Santiago. But the weather was still stormy and the sea seemed just as rough.

The next stop was Valparaiso, Chili thence northward to Callao in Peru. The ships spent Christmas at sea arriving on December 26th. Each country tried to outdo the others with entertainment for the men of the flotilla. While the ships were in Callao, a delegation of Cuban citizens, who lived in the area, presented a gold medal to the *Oregon* commemorating its service in the Spanish War. New Year's Day, 1899, was spent at Callao.

On the 9th of January 1899, the President of Peru visited the ships where official friendly exchanges were made then the flotilla sailed for the Galapagos Islands.

---

* The *USS Iris* was a steamship that the Navy refitted as a distillery ship for converting sea water to fresh water. With the American occupation of the Philippines, it was immediately obvious there had been no effective public health standards under the Spanish. As Victor Heiser M. D., a U. S. Public Health Service physician in Manila reported in 1902, the Philippines was a scene of disease, "filth and squalor." The *Iris,* as the source of clean drinking water, filled a major role for Americans there. See bibliography for Heiser's book.

64

Before the squadron reached the islands it was disbanded. The *Iowa*, in need of repairs, was ordered to Mare Island Navy Yard in San Pablo Bay, northwest of San Francisco. The *Celtic, Justin, Scindia* would accompany her.

The *Iris* (Lt. Arthur B. Conner), 1,923 tons, could make 10 knots. She and the *Oregon* proceeded into the setting sun for the Philippines with stops at Honolulu then at Guam.*

Just at sunset on March 18, 1899, the *Oregon* and the *Iris* arrived in Manila Bay. The ships at anchor and troops on parade were standing for the daily "Retreat" ceremony of lowering the flat with band, bugle and with guns firing. The battleship saluted Admiral Dewey then dropped anchor in the harbor amid the cheers of all the troops and sailors. ✛

Radio Had Not Yet Been Invented

When the war was declared while the battleship *Oregon* was at sea on the long voyage around South America, these were the days before the invention of radio. The ship had no contact with other ships or with Navy headquarters in Washington, D.C., so people throughout the country experienced great stress for the safety of the warship and its crew. For weeks at a time, the location and conditions on the battleship were unknown. When the magnificent fighting machine arrived on the Atlantic coast of the United States, unharmed and ready for action, the nationwide anxiety was relieved. The achievement was hailed as a supreme test of the efficiency of American manufacturing and seamanship.

---

* Guam was taken from Spain as part of the Spanish-American War on June 20, 1898 when the American cruiser *Charleston* (Captain Henry Glass), steamed in to Port San Luis d'Apra then fired on the fort. The Spanish Captain of the Port, Lt. Guiterrez, put out from shore and approached the warship with the acclimation: "Will you pardon our not immediately replying to your salute but we are not accustomed to receiving salutes here, and are not supplied with proper guns for returning them." He asked the reason for the warship's visit and was then told of the war which he did not know about. He surrendered his outpost immediately. The next day, Captain Glass ordered his ship's Stars and Stripes hoisted above the fort thereby taking possession of Guam in the name of the United States of America. He took aboard Guam's 60-man Spanish force then returned to Manila. Guam would quickly become a major transpacific cable relay station and port-of-transit for ships. In the 1930's, Pan American Airways "clipper" flying boats, between the U. S. mainland and the Philippines stopped at Guam.

65

Stern capstan, the 13" guns and the deck of the *Oregon*. The deck was laid with hardwood carefully mortised at every edge. (Lower) Part of the crew in tropical whites on deck in Manila Bay.

5. Philippine Adventure

The *Oregon* had made the voyage from Honolulu without incident and arrived in as perfect condition as when she made her famous trip around South America on the way to the Battle of Santiago de Cuba.

A cablegram was sent to the Navy Department:

MANILA. MARCH 19 1899. — THE OREGON AND THE IRIS ARRIVED TODAY. THE OREGON IS IN FIT CONDITION FOR ANY DUTY. DEWEY.

The *Oregon* was assigned blockade duty in Manila Bay with gunboats *Samar* and *Urdaneta* as her tenders. On May 20th, Admiral Dewey took ship for the United States with Captain Barker, of the battleship, now also commanding the naval station. He hoisted a pennant on the *Oregon* "Senior Officer Present." On the 29th, Barker was relieved of command of the ship with the arrival of Captain George F. F. Wilde.

On June 11 the *Oregon* was dispatched to Lingayan Bay to relieve the *Concord* which needed repairs. While there, two days later, a large boat expedition for relief of the gunboat *Paragua* that had run aground in the gulf and was being attacked by insurgents was sent. After this incident, the battleship went back to Manila Bay to reassume its position in the blockade.

Come August 24th, the warship went to Iloilo to assume the position of station ship. She stayed there until October when on the 24th the *Oregon* steamed back to Manila Bay. Next, the ship left for Hong Kong for docking. By November 8th, the ship was again in Lingayen Gulf where she landed a large number of her crew to assist the army, under General Wheaton, with his occupation of that place.

The *Oregon* was again involved with another landing assault when on November 26th, it put ashore 201 of its crew, under direct command of Lt. Commander Alexander McCrackin, at Vigan. This force captured Vigan without resistance and took 89

Spanish prisoners. These men were temporarily incarcerated on the deck of the battleship for the return to Manila.

On the 10th of December, the ship was ordered to Subic Bay where a detachment of her Marines were transferred to be permanently stationed there. Following this detail, the battleship went back to Manila Bay where she remained on station duty until February 1900.✣

Before returning to the Pacific, the *Oregon* went into drydock in the Brooklyn Navy Yard for extensive servicing.

6. Asiatic Patrols and Troubles

The battleship *Oregon* went to Yokohama where, on April 18, 1900, Rear Admiral Louis Kempff hoisted his flag as 2nd in command of the Asiatic Station. On the April 26th, the flag was transferred to the *Newark*, an armored cruiser, but the *Oregon* stayed in Japanese waters until May 26th. On the 24th day of May, Captain John T. Myers and 25 Marines of the battleship's Marine force were transferred to the *Newark*. This combined unit of Marines were then sent to Peking, China as legation guards. In the last days of May, the *Oregon* sailed for Hong Kong where she docked.

On account of the Boxer Rebellion, the *Oregon* was ordered, on June 23rd, to proceed to Taku, China.

The morning of June 28th was cold and foggy. While navigating through a shortcut, crew members were jolted to attention and suddenly realized:

The way to ruin a perfectly nice day is to wreck your ship!

In the Gulf of Pechili (later renamed Po Hai), the *USS Oregon* had wrenched to a stop on Pinnacle Rock that was hidden in the fog. The location was near Howki Lighthouse. For five days the ship, taking on water and listing to port stayed where it was. Finally, on July 5th, it refloated and put in to Hopegh Sound for limited inspection.

With a convoy of two ships, the battleship proceeded to the Kure Naval Ship yard at Kobe where there was a dry dock big enough to contain it. The experience in Kure had its lighter moments but was edgy for both the Japanese and the Americans for such an encounter had never occurred before. While publicly there were official smiles and indeed the Japanese had an excellent facility and able workers, it was plain that the presence of the American man-of-war was an intrusion.*

---

* For many years is was policy that the below-the-water line area of Navy ships was not

"The way to ruin a perfectly nice day is to wreck your ship!"

Battleship *Oregon*, her hull run through on an uncharted pinnacle in the Straits of Pechili ("Str. of Chih-li" on this 1906 map). The ship was on the way to Taku.

Admiral Tatsuo Tsukuduo, who retired from the Japanese Maritime Self-Defense Force (Navy) wrote to the author:

USS Oregon cruised in Bohai Gulf, North China to support the allied forces including U. S. Marine Corp resisting the Boxer mutiny in summer 1900. During the operations she touched the reef in dense fog and damaged her bottom. She sailed to Kure to repair the damage in the dry-dock of the Naval Shipyard there and stayed about one month.

The Hiroshima newspaper, *Chugoku*, published a number of reports.

●米國軍艦オレゴル

しに商船は共に今猶碇泊中なり

位なりさ御同艦を護衛し來れり一同報知艦一隻拼

幽にして彼早々石炭等の陸揚に着手せん該船渠に入るを得る

渠したるを以て多分今二十日入渠する都合にて着

米國軍艦オレゴルは別項の如く我が呉軍港に來着せしか

十七日午後一時ヽ呉軍港に來着せし

ARRIVAL OF THE US WARSHIP

July 20, 1900. Friday. - It is reported that the injured USS "Oregon" which arrived at Kure 17th afternoon, will dock perhaps on 20th, and began to unload coal immediately after her arrival.

She displaces 10,200 ton. The hull is so long that she can narrowly enter the No.1 dock. A US dispatch vessel and a merchant ship which escorted the "Oregon" are still in Kure port.

photographed except by U. S. officials. This was so foreigners would not know of some unique constructions. The *Oregon* had the uniqueness of the special keel to help stability in rough seas. While in dry-dock at Kure Naval base, the Japanese had the unique opportunity of examining the ship's bottom and keel carefully. The Japanese need for the dry-dock is clearly seen with the realization that Japan had built a number of battleships about the same time as the *Oregon*. These were the *Fuji* (launched 1896, scrapped 1948); *Yashima* (launched 1896, lost in Russo-Japanese War 1904); *Shikishima* (launched 1898, scrapped 1947); *Hatsuse* (launched 1899, lost in Russo-Japanese War 1904); *Asahi* (launched 1899, torpedoed by U.S. submarine May 1942). All were considerably heavier than the *Oregon* (10,228 tons) ranging from 12,533 to 15,453 tons. They were equipped with 12-inch guns. The U.S. had only one Spanish-American War era battleship (*Oregon*) in WWII. Of like vintage the Japanese has 5. —Editor

●米鑑の入渠に就て

清國沿海に於て座州に損傷を受けたる米國軍鑑オレゴン號は既報く修繕の爲め吳軍港に入港したるが共同鑑々に入るゝは多分本日なるべく而して溺港後は詞難夜交代にて間斷なく揚水に從事し昨日漸れを終れり聞く遊に依ればオレゴンは日本軍我搆造を異にし居れるを以て之れを入渠せしむには船渠底の盤木を取替へざる可からずと偶ほ燃は大砲を積載したる儘人渠せん蕃なれども斯ては充分の修繕をなす能はず依く問鑑長は大砲を下すべきや否やに付き目下未國政府に照會中なりと云ふ

THE DRYDOCKING OF THE US WARSHIP

July 24, 1900. Tuesday. - The "Oregon" will perhaps dock today. After it arrived at Kure, her crew pumped out the flooded sea water day and night by shifts, and it at last finished the work yesterday.

It is said that as the structure of the "Oregon" differs from the Japanese battleships, the shipyard must change the blocks of the dock. Her captain hopes to dock with out unloading her gun mounts.

Although, as it is difficult to repair completely with gun mounts, it is reported that her captain is now consulting with the US Naval Authority whether her gun mounts should be unloaded or not.

AMERICAN SAILORS VISIT HIROSHIMA

July 28, 1900. Saturday. - The sailors and marines of the USS "Oregon" which is now drydocking at Kure Naval Shipyard, allowed five days leave since 26th, Thursday.

They are visiting Hiroshima or Osaka-Kobe area during their leaves. Here, in Hiroshima, they go around the street by "Rickshaw," by bicycle, or on foot. Yesterday, some of them visited the military barracks here.

THE REPAIR OF THE "OREGON"

August 3, 1900. Friday. - The "Oregon" is receiving investigation to the damage after the dock was dried up. The injures are more severe than expected.

The aperture is large enough to allow a man to go through, furthermore, there are many depressions totals more than thirty feet in length. It is estimated to need about six months to be repaired completely.

But, since such long time occupation of the dry-dock will impede Japanese warships' maintenance schedule, it is reported that the shipyard will only perform temporary repair, and the real repair should be carried out after her going back to U.S. mainland.

The temporary repair needs some forty days, so it will be finished before thirty days hereafter.

The money which she will pay to the Japanese government for the docking charge equivalents to average 2,000 yen per day, it is estimated.

THE REPAIR CHARGE OF THE "OREGON"

August 12, 1900. Sunday. - The European allied war history shows that some countries receive such charge but others repair by good will.

As the charge may not be much money, it scarcely will become a serious question, but the Japanese government's policy is not yet set as a diplomatic problem.

Who Paid the Bill?

Referring to the newspaper article dated August 3, 1900: In the last two lines is mention of the estimated costs for the repair, and in the article of August 12 is a question about Japanese policy on who pays or is the work a courtesy?

It was no doubt an embarrassment to the Japanerse when the work proved faulty and the dry-dock had to be "dried up" again and the job done over. Inquiries in 1993 and again in early 1994 of the U. S. Navy History Center and to the National Archives, brought letters stating there is no information found in these resources regarding who paid for the repairs done in the Japanese shipyard. Or, due to the mishap of faulty initial repair, was there, plausibly, a polite bowing by the Japanese who then said the work would be done "no charge."

Many historical sources of American authorship say in words to the effect that after repairs in Japan, the ship went about its duty. This suggests that the Japanese repairs were of a permanent nature. But the battleship had to be fixed again, a few months later, in Hong Kong, then all the repair had to be done still again in the USA within a year.

Note: The *Currency Conversion Table* shows the exchange rate as 2¥ = 1 US gold $. –Editor

THE FAILURE OF THE REPAIR

August 22, 1900. Wednesday. - The USS "Oregon" which is undergoing repair at Kure Navy Yard since 24th July, hurries up the work. As mentioned previously, the gun mounts and other loads were not removed and her crew live on board the ship during her dry-docking.

The temporary repair work, it is said, is to recover the damaged bottom by wood timbers and cover them by steel plate. The real repair will be made after coming back to home land.

When the temporary work finished on 17th August, the shipyard began to flood the dry-dock after the regular arrangement. But, because much sea water leaked in through the repaired parts, the dock was dried up again, and the repair work is repeated in days and nights. She may be unable to go out from the dock before two-weeks.

Her crew had leaves since her drydocking and many of them traveled as far as Kyoto, Osaka, Kobe area. At present about five hundred crew of the original 890 remains on board the ship.

As almost of them consumed up their money, they were dispirited recently. But they seem restored pep very much because yesterday was their regular pay day, so the red-light districts may be crowded again.

USS OREGON COMPLETES REPAIR

August 29, 1900 Wednesday - The USS "Oregon" which was under repair in the Kure Navy Shipyard, got out of the dock on 26th, Sunday, after the repair work was proved to be successful. She is still stays in Kure port [being observed for some days].

With temporary repairs making the battleship seaworthy again, she was next ordered to the mouth of the Woosung River, China, where the *Oregon* was to remain as station ship for American interests in the area. The ship stayed until February 1901. On the 15th of January Captain Wilde was relieved of command by Captain Francis W. Dickins. On the 22nd of February, the vessel was ordered to proceed to Hong Kong as the ship's bottom needed further attention.

On April 5, 1901, Captain Dickins was put on detached service and ordered to return to the United States. Lieutenant Commander Charles A. Adams assumed the helm. Cdr. Adams was the first officer below the rank of Captain to command the *USS Oregon*. But there would be others. (See Appendix A) His command lasted only two days until the arrival of Captain Charles M. Thomas on the 7th.

Due to its continuing leaky bottom, the battleship was ordered to proceed to the Puget Sound Navy Yard at Bremerton on May 5th. The voyage got under way amid much cheering by the crew who were glad to shake the dust of the orient from their shoes.

While the ship was in mid-ocean, between China and Hawaii, it was struck by a typhoon. The navigator had notified the captain that the "glass was dropping" thus the command new of the weather conditions. The crew was ordered to tie down everything thus the ship sustained very little damage in the thunderous seas.

The ship put in to Mare Island Navy Yard near San Francisco then went to Bremerton for its overhaul. ✛

The Battleship *Oregon* in dry-dock at Puget Sound Navy Yard, Bremerton, Washington.

The Battleship *Oregon* in dry-dock at
Mare Island Navy Yard, Vallejo, California.

7. West Coast Patrols

The battleship entered the Puget Sound Navy Yard on April 26, 1906 where it was placed out of commission on the 27th and her personnel transferred. This dry-docking was for extensive up-grading, modification and the addition of cage mast. Her turrets were re-worked along with complete emptying and cleaning of all the coal bunkers. Special attention was given to a search for any evidence of scars from smoldering coal fires in the past. When the work was completed, the ship was placed in commission in reserve on August 29th, 1911 then attached to the Pacific Reserve Squadron. Captain Charles F. Pond commanded the ship as well as the squadron.

On October 23, 1911, the *Oregon* left Bremerton for San Diego where, on October 28th, Captain Pond reported with his ship to the Commander in Chief of the Pacific Fleet for temporary duty. The flotilla was dispatched to San Pedro to take part in a mobilization of warships to be reviewed by a delegation from the Congress of the United States. The *Oregon* was the vessel opened for visitors. On November 2, nearly 10,000 persons walked the decks of this famous war-fighter recalling its glorious action at the Battle of Santiago de Cuba.

Ports of call along the Southern California coast keep the ship's personnel occupied for the rest of November with the vessel returning to San Francisco on the 27th. Here the vessel was detached from the Pacific Fleet.

She steamed out through the Golden Gate on December 1st again for Puget Sound Navy Yard and rejoined the Pacific Reserve Squadron on December 4th.

On March 25, 1912, Captain Pond was detached from his ship and from the Pacific Reserve Fleet. Then started a hop-scotch of jumping and musical-chairs as officers of the Navy were moving on and off the battleship for varied periods of time. In 1912 the ship billeted six different commanders.

Lt. Commander Charles T. Owens assumed command of the battleship keeping it until April 13th when he too was detached. With his move, Lieutenant (jg) William H. Beehler became the *Oregon's* commanding officer – the lowest rank for a commander to this time. Three days later, on the 16th, he relinquished the bridge to Lt. Edison E. Scranton. Twelve days later, Lt. Commander Henry N. Jensen assumed command for a voyage to Tacoma to take part in a 4th-of-July event then leave the Sound for a voyage to the Columbia River.

Various newspaper accounts announced that the battleship would proceed up the river 100 miles to Portland. But no evidence of such a visit to Portland has been located. A story in the *Oregonian* said the trip was cancelled. But the Oregon did drop anchor off Astoria. The ship entertained many visitors and at least one of them is suspected of having spirited a piece of the ship's equipment from the vessel as a souvenier. It seems an odd choice of something to "liberate" – a coal shovel!

* * *

From here the battleship went back to the Straits of Juan de Fuca and to Seattle. There, on July 20th, Lt. Commander James J. Raby assumed temporary command when he relieved Lt. Cdr. Jensen. Next, the *Oregon* took its old parking place in the Puget Sound Navy Yard at Bremerton on July 22. Two day later, July 24th, Lt. Edison E. Scranton again assumed command.

On March 1, 1913, a new dry-dock at Bremerton was dedicated by a platoon of distinguished visitors including Governor Ernest Lister of Washington State. The battleship *Oregon* was docked during the dedication ceremony being the first vessel to enter the new facility.

Lt. Scranton was detached on July 2, 1913 and Lt. Cdr. Henry N. Jenson started his second tour as commander. His job lasted just one day when he surrendered his ship to Commander Charles J. Lang who held the command for 8 days.

On the 22nd of July, Lt. Cdr. Jenson again took command for another two days when on the 24th, Lieutenant (jg) Frank P. King became commander.

The *Oregon* stayed at the Navy Yard at Bremerton in reserve until about the middle of January 1915 when it left Puget Sound

The *Oregon* is the first battleship to use the new dry-dock at Bremerton.

for San Francisco. The ship had been ordered to become an open-to-the-public exhibit at the Panama-Pacific International Exposition which opened on February 20th.

Once through the Golden Gate, the battleship anchored off the exposition grounds along the city's north shore Marina District.*

When the fair closed, the battleship *Oregon* was retained as a part of the Pacific Reserve Fleet but was assigned for duty with the Naval Militia of California. She was docked at San Francisco in full commission in the reserve until April 7, 1917.

On May 8, 1916, Commander Reeves was relieved of his duty and was replaced by Commander G. W. Williams. There was another rapid succession of changes in ship captains (See Appendix A). ✤

* Not far from today's Fisherman's Wharf. At that time this was a good distance from what was considered "the city." The Municipal Railway (street car lines) had built tracks to the fair grounds and on opening day alone carried 265,000 (5¢) fare-paying passengers to the fair. The numbers of fair-goers to visit the battleship on the first day does not seem to be recorded but a witness told the author that the little boats going to the ship, both Navy whale boats (free) and private "taxi" boats (50¢ round trip), were lined up stem-to-stern hauling visitors as fast as the people could be accommodated.

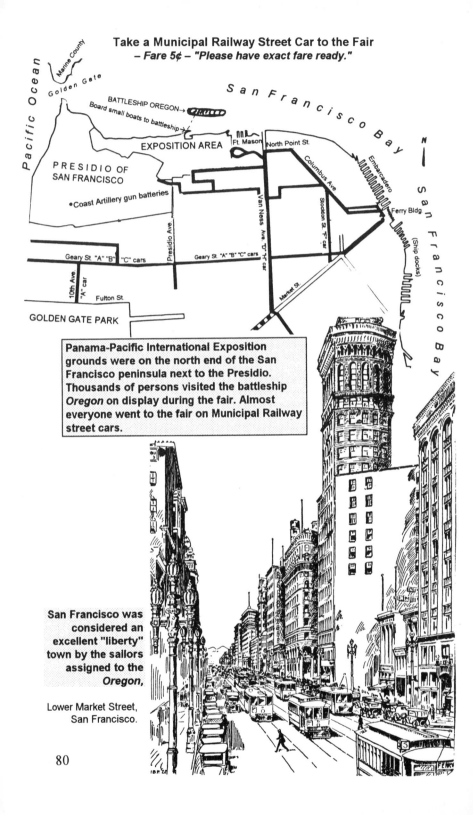

Take a Municipal Railway Street Car to the Fair
– Fare 5¢ – "Please have exact fare ready."

Pacific Ocean

Marin County

Golden Gate

San Francisco Bay

BATTLESHIP OREGON→
Board small boats to battleship→

EXPOSITION AREA

Ft. Mason   North Point St.

PRESIDIO OF
SAN FRANCISCO

•Coast Artillery gun batteries

Columbus Ave

Embarcadero

Van Ness Ave.

Stockton St. "F" car

Ferry Bldg

(Ship docks)

San Francisco Bay

Presidio Ave.

Geary St. "A" "B" "C" cars   Geary St. "A" "B" "C" cars "D" "H" car

10th Ave. "A" Car

Fulton St.

Market St.

GOLDEN GATE PARK

Panama-Pacific International Exposition
grounds were on the north end of the San
Francisco peninsula next to the Presidio.
Thousands of persons visited the battleship
Oregon on display during the fair. Almost
everyone went to the fair on Municipal Railway
street cars.

San Francisco was
considered an
excellent "liberty"
town by the sailors
assigned to the
Oregon,

Lower Market Street,
San Francisco.

Stern view of battleship *Oregon* when anchored off Astoria at mouth of Columbia River.

(Right-above) Stern deck of *Oregon* photographed about 1937 by Sam Foster probably with a No. 127 Baby Brownie Special box camera. After WWII, Sam spent a career as a newspaper and television photographer and writer in Seaside, Oregon.

(Top and lower) Stern and bow views of 13" guns that pounded the Spanish fleet at Santiago on July 3, 1898.

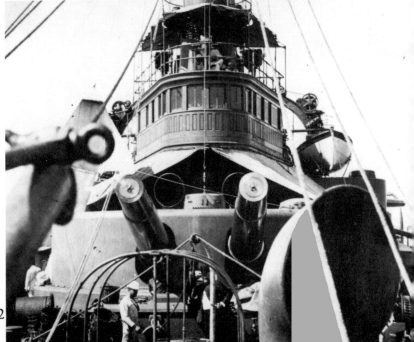

8. Interim Duty

The 6th of July 1902 found the ship at Bremerton where it remained until the 7th of September. While there, the *Oregon* underwent general overhauling. This started from the bottom and ended with the mast tip. A section of hull had to be fabricated to replace the temporary repairs made in Kure.

The ship remained in Pacific Northwest waters until February 10, 1903 when it left for San Francisco. All of the ports in the vicinity of San Francisco are considered good liberty ports by the crew therefore, those who were not pulling work details on board left the ship on leaves of up top 72 hours.

Those crew members still assigned to the ship after the China excursion felt they had done their duty in Asiatic ports. But they were in for a surprise. On November 1, 1903, the battleship *Oregon* again left the United States this time for Yokohama. On arrival there on December 18th, she joined other naval vessels of the Asiatic Station. ✛

U.S.S. Oregon

83

9. The Orient Again

During the next three years, the battleship cruised in Chinese, Japanese and Philippine waters "showing the flag" at ports-of-call. Every place the ship stopped, liberty parties went ashore where the natives welcomed them and their Yankee Dollars.*

On August 4, 1904, Captain Burwell was relieved of command when Captain John P. Merrell came aboard.

> The battleship *Oregon* won the Battleship Gunnery Trophy for excellence in target shooting in 1904 and again in 1905.

On March 8, 1906 the *Oregon* was detached from the Asiatic Station Squadron with orders for Bremerton for another dry-docking. Servicing of these ships in the navy yards was, loosely speaking, somewhat akin to running an automobile on to a rack to change the oil and rotate the tires. After several years at sea, the barnacle growth alone resulting in loss of sea-efficiency, was enough to call for a sojourn in a fresh water port, where the sea life would drop off, or else a bottom-scraping in a dry-dock.✣

The Presentation Sword

After the Battle of Santiago, contributions were received from the people of Oregon and a $1,100 gold sword was manufactured in Portland and sent to Captain Clark. Years later he presented it to the Historical Society of Vermont, his native state. It is exhibited in the State House in Montpelier near a painting of the Admiral.

---

* Fraternization between American Army and Navy men with women in the orient left many thousands of illegitimate children but there does not seem to be any data fingering sailors from the *USS Oregon* for leaving pregnant women in the various ports. In the Philippines, the situation was so severe that the American government provided money annually for many years to help with the support of these children.

The *Oregon* in the orient.
Location not identified.

10. First World War

During the First World War, the United States Government decided to be a part of a multi-national force in Siberia.* On July 30, 1918, U. S. Marines landed from the *USS New Orleans* at a bay near Vladivostok to protect American interests.

The battleship *Oregon* was selected to be a part of the operation. She was ordered to San Francisco where, with the gunboat *Vicksburg,* she was to provide protection from German submarines for the troopship *Thomas* that carried Commanding General William S. Graves, 39 officers and 1,889 soldiers. The convoy sailed on August 14, 1918. Graves mentions the slowness of the *Oregon* thus by noon of the very first day out "I directed we wave good-bye and steam full ahead for Vladivostok."

Any further role the *Oregon* may have played in the "Siberian intervention" is elusive. Falk verifies that the impatient General Graves, ordered the escorts to be thanked and dropped astern – "dismissed at sea." The *Oregon* went back to San Francisco. This was as close to any "action" the *Oregon* would see other than limited Pacific Coast patrol duty. The *Oregon,* once the glamour ship of the Spanish-American war, was getting along in years and her usefulness to the naval service was being questioned. Even though the war in Europe and in the Atlantic was hot, there was risk that German naval units might be prowling the Pacific. (Such was the case in the Marianas.) The fact that the Americans stationed a battleship, the *Oregon,* on the Pacific coast was presumed a detriment if the Germans decided to show their hand in the North Pacific Ocean. The *Oregon* did her duty but this duty did not make headlines. ✛

---

*This action was titled "American Siberian Expeditionary Forces." Only a few thousand men of the forces were to be sent by the United States. This unit was to support the Checho-Slovaks already there and to act as guards at Vladivostok to protect the Trans-Siberian railroad from being taken by the Bolsheviks. Also, to remain neutral – take no part in the political struggle

There were no famous battles and no glory but there were American casualties. There was confusion, misinformation, frostbite, dysentery, bad morale, and the Vladivostok "guard duty" reached about 2,000 miles – all the way to Irkutsk. Former Sergeant Robert W. Travis, a veteran from McMinnville, Oregon, recalled that this was not a happy duty. The article in which Sgt. Travis was interviewed by Leaverett Richards in the *Oregonian* is cited in the bibliography.

11. Post-War Doldrums Then a Grand Review

In the spring of 1919, there was some intrigue concerning work to be done on the *Oregon* to make her fit for duty as relief for the *USS Brooklyn* and become flagship of the Asiatic Fleet. An official letter from the *Brooklyn*, on station at Shanghai, China, dated 28 April 1919, reported:

> The Commander-in-Chief has noted in the public print, news items to the effect that the *USS Oregon* was being fitted out at Mare Island Navy Yard for duty as the relief of the *USS Brooklyn* and [to become the] Flagship of the Asiatic Station. While no official notice of such change had been received ... the persistence [of the] rumor continues to circulate that the *Brooklyn* is about to return to the United States, impels him to bring the matter to the [Navy] Department's attention.

The letter went on to say there was no known reason why the *Brooklyn* should be withdrawn and that the *Brooklyn*, being in "satisfactory and serviceable" condition, be continued as Flagship of the Asiatic Fleet. The Commander, R. R. Rogers, declared, concerning the *Oregon*:

> The service requirements and climatic conditions on this station are such as to make the *Oregon* wholly unsuited for duty as the flagship of the station as her quarters for officers and men are small and badly ventilated, her steam turrets make her hot and her steaming radius and speed are not great. The Commander-in-Chief is frequently confronted with he necessity of entertaining large parties of foreign diplomatic and military representatives and to that end requires more quarters and accommodations than could be made available upon the *Oregon*.

It is observable that Mr. Rogers had not looked into the *Oregon's* history to recognize that the ship had been "entertaining large parties..." while on Asiatic stations a couple of decades earlier. It appears that the station commandant, comfortable with his flag on the *Brooklyn*, at an excellent duty-port, Shanghai, did not want his lifestyle challenged by the presense of the *Oregon*

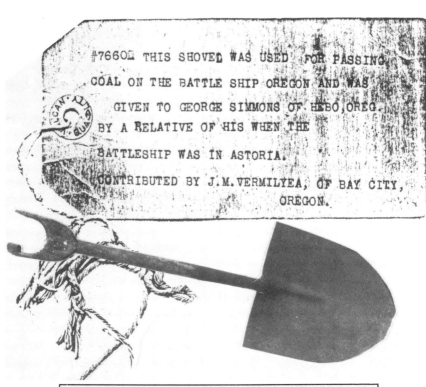

#76602 THIS SHOVEL WAS USED FOR PASSING COAL ON THE BATTLE SHIP OREGON AND WAS GIVEN TO GEORGE SIMMONS OF HEBO, OREG. BY A RELATIVE OF HIS WHEN THE BATTLESHIP WAS IN ASTORIA. CONTRIBUTED BY J.M.VERMILYEA, OF BAY CITY, OREGON.

There must he dozens of artifacts from the Battleship *Oregon* in museums and in private collections. This coal shovel is in Tillamook Pioneer Museum, Tillamook, Oregon.

which would obviously disturb it.

Within a few weeks the Battleship *Oregon* put in to the Puget Sound Navy Yard at Bremerton. Here, on June 12, 1919, she was decommissioned. But life for the old vessel was not yet over.

*   *   *

On August 21st, the ship was recommissioned for a special purpose. She was to be the ship on which President Woodrow Wilson would review the Pacific Fleet that would pass in review for the President in Puget Sound.

The Presidential train arrived in Tacoma on September 13. The President spoke to huge crowds in a stadium and in the Armory. Back on the train, he went to Seattle where his reception was the greatest and warmest every accorded an individual visiting the city to that time. Every hotel was full and there were a reported 5,000 people sleeping in the parks.

The Secretary of the Navy, and Mrs, Daniels, welcomed the

president and as soon as the party reached the dock, they were to board a launch that would carry them to the *Oregon*.

The President's wife, Edith Bolling Wilson, vividly recalled:

Secretary of the Navy and Mrs. Daniels were at the station to greet us when we arrived, and we drove through thronged streets to the dock. The barge of Admiral Hugh Rodman was expected to be ready to convey the reviewing party to the historic battleship *Oregon*. But by some negligence the barge was not there. Commander Foote, personal aide to the Secretary of the Navy, promptly took over a naval launch, and we got aboard. With Secretary and Mrs. Daniels, Secret Service men, aides, reporters, etc., we constituted a large party. As Commander Foote ordered the launch shoved off, the small craft heeled over until the port rail was nearly under water. Then we ran bow-on into another launch. Personally I would not have excused the officers who had endangered lives in this way, though the President did.

After the party reached the *Oregon,* everyone clamored aboard. Then the *Oregon* passed slowly by the paral-lel lines of the great Navy ships each of which would fire its guns in salute to Mr. President who was the Commander in Chief.

The old battleship moved down the Bay, passing the *New Mexico, Mississippi, Idaho, Texas and New York*. From each roared salvos of 21-guns, while above us circled airships. Then came 27 destroyers spaced about three hundred yards apart, followed by every type of vessel – destroyers, tugs, submarine chasers, etc. On each vessel the sailors lined the rail at attention. The bands flung across the waters strains of the National Anthem.

The review over, we went to the Hotel Washington. I was glad to get back to our suite on the top floor of the hotel which overlooked the harbor. Straight out as far as the eye could see lay the entire fleet, every ship ablaze with [search]lights playing the sky. Surely America should have been proud of such a sight. It awed us both as we sat on a little roof garden and gazed silently.

Indeed.

Following this dress parade for the president, the grand battleship was fully decommissioned on October 4, 1919.

On July 1, 1920, the *Oregon* was officially designated "BB-3" in the Navy's new way of designating its ships. "BB" stood for battleship. BB-1 was the *Indiana* and BB-2 the *Massachusetts*. BB-4 was the *Iowa* also of Spanish War participation.

In 1920, the ship was considered to have outlived its usefulness and incapable of any warlike operations therefore plans were considered to scrap her. ✢

The *Oregon*

Ruth Coffee Hills

Morning, off the coast of Cuba;
    Ships at anchor, lying tense;
Waiting for some sign or signal
    That would break the long suspense.

Since the fall of Santiago
    And the coming of our fleet,
Spanish ships within the harbor
    Saw no way of safe retreat.
Then Cervera, under orders,
    Took his only chance to win;
Made a noble dash for freedom
    Past the ships that hemmed them in.

"Speed to westward, "cried Cervera,
    "Sink the *Brooklyn* and we've won."
Racing on to aid the *Brooklyn*,
    Leaping like a thing possessed,
Passed the *Iowa* and *Texas,*
    Far outdistanced our the rest.

Racing while her guns were speaking;
    Spanish ships were falling back
Powerless to withstand the fury
    Of the *Oregon's* attack.

Still one ship was left, the *Colon*:
    But the *Oregon* sped on.
Overtook and turned her backward,
    And the victory was won.

Modest when her task was finished,
    Giving honor to the rest.
Ready when her country called her,
    Oregon had stood the test.

Home at last in quiet waters
    Of the State whose name she bore
When she clothed herself with glory
    Off that distant Cuban shore.

Shall we grudge her care and shelter,
    Now her fighting days are done?
Rather, let us bow before her,
    Ship of pride, the *Oregon.*

The government may, from time-to-time, build bigger and
more powerful battleships than the *Oregon*, but they
could never build a better one.
—Cora A. Thompson, Secty., Battleship *Oregon* Commission

12. Oregon's Floating Monument

The Navy determined that the *Oregon* had outlived its usefulness so it was listed to be scrapped. However, Franklin D. Roosevelt, then Assistant Secretary of the Navy, intervened and the ship was saved – for awhile. It remained tied up at Bremerton.

Then plans for breaking up the *Oregon* hit the newspapers once again. This time it was due to the political considerations that resulted from the Washington Naval Treaty in 1922. (See Appendix H.) While the public did not seem overly interested in the implications of the treaty and the formula concerning which nations would be allowed to build what kind and size of fighting ships, there was outrage, once again, at any thought of breaking up the good old *Oregon*. Public indignation grew to fever pitch and at the insistence of Hon. Charles E. Hughes, the battleship was excluded from the scrapping order.

In 1923, the state legislature passed an act allowing the state to take over the vessel from the federal government. It appropriated $15,000 a year for maintenance. The Navy estimated its costs to prepare and deliver the ship at $20,000. The City of Portland agreed to provide suitable access, a well-built passageway to the ship and to perpetually provide power and water.

In 1925, the citizens of *Oregon* requested their Governor to ask that the ship be moored in the Willamette River, at Portland, as a floating monument. There was considerable give and take – some citizens of Oregon were adamantly against the idea – nevertheless, after considerable discussion, the Navy, on June 25, 1925, with the provisions of the 1923 act in hand, agreed. But there were stipulations. It was understood that the *Oregon* would remain the property of the federal government – just on loan to the state. The state agreed.

On July 14, 1925, she was delivered to the State of Oregon in the harbor of Portland to be preserved as an object of historic and

The Pennant

The "Homeward Bound" pennant of the *Oregon* was flown on her triumphant return trip to the Pacific. It was approximately 268-feet long. There is about 75-feet of plain blue silk, 21-inches wide at the staff end on which 45 big white stars are appliquéed every 17-inches. The longest end is red and white which gradually tapered to a point but about 3-yards of the tip had been whipped into rags and cut off. Now the end, instead of being pointed, is just 9-inches wide at the end. From being dragged in the water for the long pennant was hard to handle, the red has faded into the white and the last white star is more red than white. The pennant was placed in the State House at Salem for a number of years until the ship started on her last long trip from Bremerton to Portland. It was placed aboard the *Oregon* when she came up the Willamette River, when it was flown officially for the last time. It was one of the most treasured trophies on board the old ship. It is some "long" job, both literally and figuratively, to roll and unroll this lengthy work of silk.

sentimental interest.

The Old Bull Dog, looking glamorous with her new paint job, was berthed at the east end of the Broadway Bridge where she remained for over ten years. But it was in a very inconvenient place being almost in the regular shipping channel. Scores of people looked down on the *Oregon*, studied the exceedingly long flight of stairs to get down to it, then the stiff walk back up all of those steps, regretable turned away without visiting one of the most historical spots of the West.

Staircase Too Threatening

When President Franklin Delano Roosevelt was taken to the east end of the Broadway Bridge, he got out of his car and looked down on this grand old warrior, but [due to his physical limitation] was unable to go aboard.   —*The Spectator.* Portland Apr. 13, 1935

The ship became a collecting place for war relics. Year by year the collection of souveniers grew and many large valuable collections began pouring in not only from every State in the Union, but from England and Canada as well. In the late 1920's it was one of the largest, if not the largest, war museums in the United States. When the museum was closed in World War II, it was estimated there were over 10,000 artifacts on exhibit.

Being fully aware of the inconvenience the long staircase was to visitors, as well as the ship sticking out into the river, in 1935, the City Council passed an ordinance giving four and one-half acres of land at the foot of West Jefferson Street, on the Willamette River, as a permanent berth for the *Oregon*.

Several years past without a move then, in 1938, the National Encampment of United Spanish War Veterans convened in Portland. One of the ceremonies was the towing of the old battleship from the Northeast end of the Broadway Bridge to the west side of the river for its permanent berth.

Originally, it was planned to tow the vessel through the raised Hawthorne Bridge and moor her immediately south of the draw bridge near the marine park. But deposits of silt had filled in the newly prepared basin. A delay was mandated due to the requirement for dredging.

The Oregon *Journal* printed a story about the move in its

The VFW was the first organization to use the ship for its home meeting place.

**Battleship *Oregon*
Naval Post 1478
Veterans of Foreign Wars
Chartered December 11, 1926**

issue of September 12, 1938 on page 1. Here are extracts from that piece:

> The *Oregon* [committee] has an eight-year old grant to tie up at her temporary position...from former owners of the public market site giving permission to moor the ship there.
>
> The lines that held her since 1925 were cut shortly after 9:20 a.m. and the stately old war dog began her slow journey upstream. The assistance of 5 tugs and the help of the harbor patrol boat *Mulkey* were needed to start and change her direction.
>
> The ship was greeted at the Public Market moorage by a large crowd among whom was an unknown bugler who sounded "colors" as the tugs began to move the vessel sidewise into the dock.

Passengers aboard the battleship were excited on being having been invited. The procession went through the Broadway, Steel and Burnside bridges easily. Those on deck held their

---

**Invited passengers on Battleship *Oregon*
when the battleship was moved in the Portland harbor.**

Roy Richardson	Mrs. C. S. Jackson
Mr. and Mrs. B. M. Heucey	John Richardson
E. A. and Earl Long	Earl Mead
Mrs. W. W. Gabriel	Mrs. Stanley Chin
Mrs. Howard Wadddell	George F. A. Walker
Jerry W. E. Hopes	O. R. Weiss
Mr. and Mrs. Ray Weston	Dean Collins
Carl Abrams	Richard Diech
Myrtle Reid	Mrs. Nelson W. Hibbs
Wallace S and Wm. Wharton	Mrs. E. Paris Zehntbauer
Mr. and Mrs. J. H. Barus	Mrs. William House
Mrs. M. Donald Spencer	Tom West
Mrs. Lee Patterson	Kathleen Walker Turner
Mrs. W. Thompson	Mrs. Mae Rose Walker
George Knudsen	Mary Lois and Marshall N. Dana

The Battleship *Oregon*, with invited guests aboard, make "voyage" across Willamette River to new berth.

breaths as the ship barely cleared the west draw of the Morrison Bridge with only a few inches of room to spare.

Probably the busiest passenger on the "voyage" was Guy A. Davis. Davis had been on the *Oregon* as a Landsman, and marine engineer on the historic trip around South America then stood duty on the ship during the Battle of Santiago de Cuba. Now he wanted to see the whole ship including his former duty stations. After the war, he had been transferred to other duty.

Davis said he had not seen the ship since he served aboard. He was the only crewman from the Spanish-American War experience who was on board the ship for the move in Portland harbor.

With about fifty passengers, including those who wrote their names on a special "guest list" document, and a single man who had been a sailor on the ship during the Battle of Santiago de Cuba in 1898, the gallant fighting ship made its first, last and only trip between points in the Portland harbor. In her new berth, the battleship would be out of danger from the channel traffic and the old dangerous stairway was eliminated.

95

The *Oregon* in her new berth on the west side of the Willamette River. (Lower) New, wide, gangplank provided easy access to the ship.

96

The *Oregon* at Portland.

A few months later, the required amount of money was raised by the spirited citizens of Portland and the State and the work on the basin and sea wall was completed. The park was designed with a solidly built railed gang plank from the street level to the deck of the battleship. She served now as a meeting place for Sea Scouts, Boy Scouts, Girl Scouts, Camp Fire Girls, 4-H-Clubs, Naval Reserve and a Navy Post of the Veterans of Foreign Wars as well as the Navy Mothers of America.

Visits to the memorial battleship were regularly scheduled for field trips by Oregon as well as Western Washington schools and for meetings of patriotic groups.

Hundreds of people visited the ship every day. There was no admission charge to military personnel in uniform or to former servicemen or army nurses. There was no charge to school-age children through high school, but those under 14 years of age had to have guardians. To all others, a 25¢ admission was charged to assist with maintenance costs.

The battleship was closed at night and its gangway barred.

*   *   *

No ship, ever, on any ocean, had been watched by the world with so much breathless interest as was the *Oregon* on her dramatic trip around South America through the Strait of Magellan, to become the "Bull Dog of the Navy" at the battle of Santiago. In miles traveled, in daily mileage made, in hazards faced and perils met and overcome, and in the final triumph of a voyage that was the sensation of the age, the ship was finely berthed as a monument in Portland. As a historical monument, it was matchless.✛

I Was There
The *Oregon* was the first to see the enemy, the first to fire a shot and the last to fire a shot at the close of the action.
—Sgt. Frederick A. Ramsey, USMC, on deck during the battle

The Battleship *Oregon*, although out of commission as a fighting monster, is still performing a wonderful service in cultivating patriotic pride and high ideals for which the Stars and Stripes have ever stood. —Willard H. Stevens, Oregon State Grange. Jan. 8, 1937

Nearly every spring during the week-long Rose Festival in Portland, there are visits of U.S. and Canadian Navy and Coast Guard ships that tie up in the Willamette River at Marine Park near where the *Oregon* was berthed. Picture was made in the 1930's during the parade of the searchlights.

The *Oregon* "Burned Rubber"
A Jack-Rabbit Start That Paid Off

As the *Brooklyn* was a faster ship than the *Oregon* by 5 knots, how could the *Oregon* outrun it in the final chase?

1) To preserve fresh water, the *Brooklyn,* and other ships, used salt water in boilers during the blockade, resulting in lower power due to scale in the boiler tubes.

2) The *Oregon,* using fresh water, and the only American ship to maintain full steam during the blockade, was capable of an instant, rapid departure.

3) The *Oregon's* use of hard coal, which burns hotter, brought the ship to full speed faster while the *Brooklyn* had only soft coal and got off to a slower start – never did catch the *Oregon*.

One might say that the Engineer of the *Oregon* was sitting at the wheel with his foot on the clutch waiting for the "light." When the light changed, being prepared, the *Oregon*"dug out – burned rubber" leaving all the other ships behind.

99

Wrong Item Saved

A figurehead, in the form of a shield, was on the bow of the *Oregon* on the long trip and through the Spanish War of 1898. In 1909, a figurehead was presented to the State of Oregon by the Navy Department. It was placed in the lobby of the old State House in Salem. When fire destroyed the State House in 1935, the shield was saved. In 1936 when the old ship was being repaired and repainted, the shield was taken out of storage with the intention of replacing it on the bow of the ship but it was to small. The shield received from the Navy did not fit a battleship. Evidently the wrong figurehead was presented to the State of Oregon. Today the shield is permanently mounted in the park alongside the Willamette River in Portland.

Salutes

In June 1933, when the motorship *Oregon* of the French Line passed the old battleship *Oregon*, berthed in the Willamette River, the Flag of the visitor was dipped in salute to the honoraable veteran of the Battle of Santiago de Cuba. The battleship returned the salute.

Mast with bow-crest shield has been a part of Battleship *Oregon* Memorial Marine Park for nearly half-a-century. But the upper-mast and cross-arm has been removed as a safety measure. Original upper-mast was wood, and was replaced with metal unit (shown) in late 1960's. Bert Webber salvaged the 10-foot base end and hauled it to Lake Oswego where it became the lower section of his home flag pole.

101

BATTLESHIP OREGON
MEMORIAL MARINE PARK

THIS IS THE MAIN MAST OF THE IMMORTAL U.S.S. OREGON. ALL THAT REMAINS OF ONE OF THE WORLD'S MOST GALLANT SHIPS, AFTER SERVING AMERICA IN THREE MAJOR WARS.

LAUNCHED IN 1893 SHE MADE THE FAMOUS RUN THROUGH THE STRAITS OF MAGELLAN IN 1898. SHE JOINED THE AMERICAN FLEET AT KEY WEST, FLORIDA AND PROCEEDED INTO THE WORLD FAMOUS BATTLE OF SANTIAGO OF THE SPANISH-AMERICAN WAR. THE "OREGON" UNDOUBTEDLY FURNISHED THE NEEDED POWER TO MAKE THIS AN OVERWHELMING AMERICAN VICTORY.

IN WORLD WAR I THE OREGON SAW DUTY AS A COAST DEFENSE AND TRAINING SHIP. AFTER A FEW YEARS IN PORTLAND HARBOR AS A MUSEUM, SHE WAS USED AS AN AMMUNITION BARGE AND DEPOT IN WORLD WAR II.

THIS BRIEF HISTORY OF THE "BULL DOG OF THE NAVY" HAS BEEN FURNISHED AS A PUBLIC SERVICE BY THE...

"NAVY LEAGUE OF THE UNITED STATES"

Battleship *Oregon* Memorial Marine Park on the Willamette River in Portland. A capsule of the ship's history was presented by the Navy League of the United States.

The mast from the *Oregon* presents
a different view from every angle.

A TRIBUTE TO ALL
U.S. MARINES
WHO SERVED ABOARD
THE
U.S.S. OREGON
DONATED BY
MARINE CORPS LEAGUE

The tribute to the Marines who had served on the ship is a small bronze plaque permanently affixed to the mast.

People of all ages visit Battleship *Oregon* Memorial Marine Park every day of the year. Large picture made in April 1994. Small picture of Lauren Webber made in 1967.

The stacks from the *Oregon* are exhibited in Liberty Ship Park about one-quarter mile downstream.

Ode to A Warrior
Colonel Clarence B. Douglas, St. Louis, wrote an ode to the battleship *Oregon* for the launching in 1893. Many years later, in Portland, he re-wrote the ode from memory and framed, it was displayed in the Master state room for years, but it finally disappeared.

The Schminck Memorial Museum, Lakeview, Oregon has these souvenirs of the *Oregon.* The chest of drawers was "Presented to the Citizens of Lake County in recognition of their outstanding War Bond purchase record for the year 1942" - January 16, 1943.

The "NO SMOKING" SIGN IS from the ship when berthed in Portland. Probably every square-inch of the ship's wood was eventually sold as souvenirs.

Remember Pearl Harbor December 7, 1941

FAREWELL TO U.S.S. OREGON

at Portland, Oregon, December 7, 1942 when famous battleship of Spanish War fame is officially turned over to the U. S. Navy by the State of Oregon to be converted into scrap to fight again for the good old U.S.A. and her allies.   "I Have Not Yet Begun To Fight"   —John Paul Jones

Special events of an historical nature bring out postal historians to record the event. Souvenir covers as this one were issued by the Pacific University Alumni Stamp Club in Forest Grove, Oregon. (Lower) Another souvenir from the *Oregon* was the entire, steel, Radio Room that was hauled to West Linn for use by Amateur Radio station W7HRV, Carl E. Braun. He was Chief Radio Operator on the ship in the First World War.

AUG 17 1948 .... OREGON CITY ENTERPRISE

Battleship Oregon Radio Shack Preserved

13. World War II – Guam

The opening guns of World War II for the United States was the Japanese attack on Pearl Harbor, December 7, 1941. President Franklin Delano Roosevelt declared to Congress the next day: "This day will live in infamy"

People in high places considered returning the battleship *Oregon* to duty. If reconditioned to anywhere near its original speed, it could serve well as convoy escort for the "Liberty" ships being mass-produced. These freighters cruised at only 6 knots. The battleship, at 13-to-25 knots, would do well, it was said.

But the grand old "bull dog," once the power-house of the American Navy, was now toothless as her engines and other vitals had been removed or purposely put out-of-service under terms of the Washington Naval Treaty of 1922. Obviously, she wasn't going anywhere under her own power. Therefore, thoughts again turned to cutting her apart for scrap iron.

Letters to the editors of newspapers show there were two sides to the issue. "If her iron is needed to make new war ships, then let her go," cried some. "Don't even *think* about destroying this monument" whaled the few veterans who were left from the Spanish War.

Even before the war started, the Navy department was thinking about the old ship because it officially changed its designation from "BB-3," a "battleship," to "IX-22" an "unclassified miscellaneous ship." The Navy had obviously not forgotten about their old war-dog, the *Oregon*.

It is not our purpose here to replay the arguments that flew back and forth between Oregon's Governor Charles A. Sprague, other politicians, and the Navy, by telegrams, airmail letters and pleading telephone calls on both sides of the issue. But in the end, the occupying historical and patriotic organizations on the ship, and all their memorial paraphernalia that had been collected and displayed there for decades, was off-loaded.

Since 1925 the ship had been on "loan" to the State of Oregon. Now, November 2, 1942, the ship was stricken from Navy inventory and transferred to Oregon State ownership. Then bids were advertised, on December 3, for breaking her up. On the 7th, the first anniversary of "the dastardly deed at Pearl Harbor,:" the *Oregon* was sold to two Portland businessmen for $35,000. They would break it up as scrap metal. But after the deal was made and the demolition started, the Navy requested that the scrapping processes stop once the work reached the main deck and after the hull's interior had been stripped.

Just before the once gallant battleship was released from its mooring in the Willamette River (March 3, 1943) and towed to the ship-wrecker in Kalama, Washington, its foremast was removed and presented to the City of Portland. *

In September, the Navy was told that the hull was ready for whatever the Navy had in mind. The first action the Navy took was to reinstate the "IX-22" designation and placed the hull back in service.

The next word about the hull was that it was supposed to be towed to Guam and sunk there to become part of a breakwater. Why tow it empty? Dynamite, tons of it, was necessary, according to the Army Engineers, for blasting jungles to clear the way for building airports that would support B-29 Superfortress bombers for raids on the home islands of Japan. The ship's hull was in good shape. Why not pack the hull full of dynamite then tow it to Guam?**

What a change for the battleship *Oregon*. In the Spanish-American War she had plowed her way through stormy seas for over 14,000 miles and arrived at destination with her big guns ready to blast the enemy. Now, as an unarmed, powerless, nothing-better-than-a-barge, she would be towed to war on the end of a rope!

* The mast, with a wooden extension for a flagpole, was later installed in the marine park along the Willamette River..

** In July 1944, the hulk had been loaded with dynamite and other various types of ammunition and was towed to Guam to be used as a floating ammunition depot.   —Annex to letter, National Archives & Records Service - Military Archives - Div. Naval; Hist. (OP-09B9) to author Dec. 14, 1972.

When the *Oregon* went to that earlier war, newspapers cried of her victories and cheered her on. But now the once "Bulldog of the Navy" had lost his teeth, his snarl, and his shape as well as his identity. The old sea-dog did not look good in his old age. In World War II, the once gallant battleship was an obscure "unclassified miscellaneous" barge that did not make headlines.

Standing out into the Pacific Ocean in July of 1944 was a tug boat, with its tow, heading toward Hawaii. Then this odd-combination turned southwest. The first stop was Eniwetok in the Marshall Islands. There had been a fierce battle in the Marshall Islands and dynamite was needed to clear ground for airports.

After the war, Val Davis, from Klamath Falls, Oregon, was proud of his Navy service and told people he had served aboard the *Oregon* during World War II.

Indeed! "Naugh, Naugh" was the jeer.

Davis wrote to the author on June 18, 1974:

I was a signalman on the *USS Caelum* (AK-106) and took the blinker message from the beach master at Eniwetok telling us to stand a 2-man continuous watch on board the *Oregon* as she was loaded with dynamite and waiting for a sea-going tug to tow her to Guam. In fact, I've had some pretty heated arguments after the war when I told people that I stood watch on the battleship *Oregon* in a World War II War Zone.

From the Marshalls, the tow boat pulled the barge across Micronesia to Guam, in the Mariana Islands, then released his charge to the Captain of the Port.

In the middle of September 1944, *USS LCI(G)-474* was ordered to guard the ex-battleship which was then moored in the lagoon of the village of Meriso in southern Guam. This was away from the active port of Apra by quite a few miles as a safety measure because of the barge's cargo. The *Oregon,* as she was still called by just about everyone, was tied to a bow anchor and by chains to a mooring buoy at the stern. The LCI was moored alongside on her port side during the 2½ months it took to complete the unloading.

The primary duty was to protect the *Oregon* from native parties and also to prevent any Japanese, which were still on the island, from making any visits to the *Oregon.*

The first night the *Oregon* was moored at Meriso, the crew of the LCI brought up a number of boxes from the hold for in-

Ex-Battleship *Oregon* (BB3) as a "flat-topped barge" (IX-22) is dwarfed by *U.S.S. Missouri* in floating dry-dock at Meriso Harbor, Guam.

spection. Just as they were opening a box, there was a burst of machine gun fire from the beach only 75 yards away. While the Marines had promised to take care of any intruders, and probably did so in this instance, the men of the LCI suddenly realized, having just opened the dynamite on deck, that it would take just one shot to blow up the ammunition, the LCI, the *Oregon* and all of them with it.

Shortly after the arrival, ComSerRon 12, the Navy organization that was supervising the *Oregon*, began sending LCTs and LCVPs into Meriso Lagoon for loads of dynamite. Much went for blasting purposes at Apra Harbor (Guam) and for use on Tinian and Siapan (B-29 airports). Later, another ship took off 100 tons of blasting powder for use on Palau. The reasons of safety in

The Navy maintained guards on the *Oregon* to thwart visits by Japanese who were still on Guam, as well as curious Chamoros.

choosing Meriso over Apra was obvious with all this traffic in high explosives.

The crew that worked aboard the *Oregon* said they did not feel much danger. It was presumed that, with prescribed safety precautions, no serious accidents would happen. Hourly temperature readings were taken in holds. Wind scoops were rigged for air circulation through all 7 hatches and there was a total embargo on smoking on this ex-battleship that was now a floating powder-keg.

There was heavy use of searchlights as all of the unloading was done at night. This was because working in the daytime on the scorching hot, steel deck of the *Oregon* was impossible. Every night, when there was a ship alongside, about 15 tons of dynamite was unloaded, by the Navy stevedore crew, into the waiting vessel. The boxes were brought to the deck with a winch. As each box emerged from the hold, it was inspected to make certain there

113

were no smashed corners or splits, then each box was carefully sent down a chute to the waiting craft.

There was never a report of any damage to the dynamite, but one of the sailors did not fare as well.

The *Oregon's* First War-Time Casualty
The log of the LCI-gunboat, for November 3, reveals a man was hurt.

A sailor was injured when he fell from the top of the open hatch on the main deck to the bottom of the hold. This was about 35 feet.

This would be the *Oregon's* first and only reported shipboard casualty during a war in three wars.

Several times the old war ship broke here moorings and had to be "rescued" and towed back to her assigned position. On one occasion, during a typically wild Guamainian typhoon (November 14-15, 1948), she broke loose and drifted to sea and could not be found. After weeks of looking, the hulk was located by search planes about 500 miles southwest of Guam in the Philippine Sea gently riding the swells. A tow boat was sent and the way-ward vessel was brought back to Meriso Lagoon.

The war over, what to do with the old ship? In a lengthy legend prepared by the Navy for use with the photograph of the hull at Port Meriso, the journalist declared:

Today Oregonians await her next assignment. It is hoped that some day the grand old warrior and survivor of three wars will find its way back to Portland where it will be assigned 'permanent' duty. Oregonians, proud of her, would like nothing better.

It didn't happen. Again the matter came up of sinking her as part of a breakwater at Cabros Island, Guam. She was already nearby. But there were more important decisions occupying military minds so the hull was left where it floated – in Meriso's harbor. The steel hull was in fine shape and could still be broken for scrap metal. Bids were called and on March 15, 1956 the Massey Supply Corporation on Guam purchased the hull from the United States Government for salvage.

The Japanese had always been in the market for scrap metal. Some say a contributing factor for the cause of the outbreak of

Hearing that the "good old Battleship *Oregon*," even having been converted to an ammunition-carrying barge, was in southern Guam, these four sailors, all from Portland, borrowed a Jeep and hustled off to find it. Left to right: Scott, Brown, Myers, Taylor. After the war, they returned to Portland.

WWII with the Japanese was that the American government, in the 1930's, had cut off the sale of scrap iron and oil to them. The hull of the *Oregon* was one mighty big piece of metal. Were the Japanese still interested in acquiring it?

The entrepreneurs at Guam made a deal with the Iwai Sanggo Company whose owners towed a now weeping old bull dog to Kawasaki, Japan.

Newspapers in the United States and in Japan* ran pictures of the now rusting and barnacle encrusted hull calling it a "gaunt hulk" and declared it was "resting at its last moorings." The Japanese ship-breakers turned the once glamour fighting ship of the world into scrap iron.✢

---

* Honolulu *Star-Bulletin* June 7, 1956. Tokyo *Asahi Evening News*, June 4, 1956

ASAHI EVENING NEWS

Canal Zone 'Inspiration' Being Scrapped in Japan

By J. B. Thomas

The ship that in a very real sense, "inspired" the Panama Canal is ending her days in Japan. A ghost of the historic 10,000-ton U.S. battleship "OREGON" (BB3, IX22) World War I Pacific Fleet Flagship, was towed into Kawasaki (Yokohama) May 21.

The powerful tug "WANDO" and herself had hauled her all the way from Guam.

Nearly 50 years had elapsed since her hero's welcome to Yokohama in 1903. Most of her will belong to history by her 60th birthday, next month. She was commissioned at San Francisco July 15, 1896.

But it now takes a strong imagination to picture her as a spotless, virginal white showpiece—all spit and polish, with tall yellow-buff stacks and flamboyant red, white and blue shield bow-crest, which made her once the cynosure of all eyes.

She cannot now be positively identified by any visible mark remaining on or in her.

The *USS Oregon* (IX-22) (x-BB3) (x-Coastal Battleship No.3) earned these medals and awards:

SPANISH AMERICAN CAMPAIGN MEDAL 20 Apr - 10 Dec 1898
PHILIPPINE CAMPAIGN MEDAL 18 Mar - 7 Oct 1899;
                                    8 Nov 1899 - 13 Feb. 1900
WORLD WAR I VICTORY MEDAL
AMERICAN DEFENSE SERVICE MEDAL
ASIATIC-PACIFIC CAMPAIGN MEDAL
WORLD WAR II VICTORY MEDAL

14. The Battleship *Oregon's* Post Office

Officers and crews aboard warships of the United States wrote letters home, and received letters, more-or-less regularly depending on conditions and where their ship was serving. From the earliest days, the men kept their letters then, with United States postage stamps affixed, placed them in a mail pouch attached to the gangplank at the foreign port-of-call. These pouches were picked up by shore personnel and dispatched to the United States usually through the diplomatic service. Sometimes a rubber stamp impression (but not a postmark) of the U. S. Embassy, showing that the letter had passed through its hands, might be applied. Often these letters bore the postmark of the city in the U. S. where the pouch was off-loaded from overseas. There were exceptions.

The original Act of Congress establishing the Navy Postal Services was approved by Congress on May 27, 1908 and went into effect with General Orders No. 74, June 27, 1908 and No. 79, November 18, 1908. Ships did not receive operating equipment – postmarking devices, Registry Journals, scales, stocks of "accountable paper" (postage stamps) –until the end of 1908 or early in 1909.

After the battleship *Oregon* arrived in the Philippines (March 18, 1899), letters from ship personnel could be mailed at the Manila postoffice bearing either Spanish or United States postage stamps. Covers (envelopes for letters) with the *Oregon* return logo in upper left corner (as illustrated here) but with Spanish stamps (acceptable) and the Manila postmark would be plausible between March 19 and June 29, 1899. Regular U. S. postage

117

**Letter from American sailor on *Oregon* bears U.S.
5¢ stamp and Manila, Philippine Islands postmark.**

stamps were available from early March. On June 30th, regular
U. S. stamps overprinted "PHILIPPINES" went on sale.

Major philatelic dealers and private collectors contacted by
the author held no covers showing the *Oregon* logo with either
Spanish and these U. S. overprinted stamps when inquiry was
made early in 1994. But one cover with a regular issue 5¢ U. S.
stamp postmarked April 9, 1899, in Manila has been discovered.

The Post Office on the *Oregon* was officially established on
April 9, 1913 and was discontinued June 7, 1919.

David A. Kent, of the Universal Ship Cancellation Society,
wrote:

Since her post office was in operation for more than six years, you would
think that postmarks from her would be common. Exactly the opposite is true
– they are the scarcest of any postmarks from our nation's battleships. Less
than a dozen are known to exist and the first was not even discovered until the
1960's.

The reason for this scarcity is not clear but it probably has to do with the
fact that she was no longer a first-line ship by 1913. She was a reserve ship
that spent most of her time tied up to a pier rather than at sea on operations.
Most likely the mail clerk rarely operated his post office and crew members
found it easier to drop letters in the mail box on the pier than bother the mail
clerk.

Kent wrote that even with the rarity of *Oregon* postmarks,
there were three different types discovered. One is a 4-bar
postmark of 1912. There is a second in a double-circle for use on

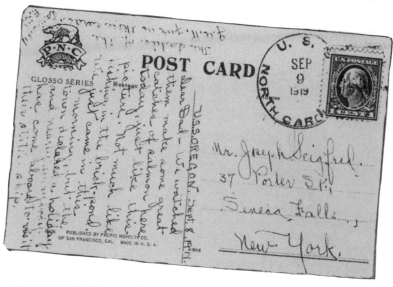

(Top) Special cover from Battleship *Oregon* mailed at the post office on *U.S.S. Memphis* shows that the *Memphis* was in Portland on July 19, 1937. The "PORTLAND" and "OREGON" in the postmark are hand-set type and are changed depending on where the ship is at the time of mailing. (Lower) A card from a sailor on the *Oregon* was sent with other mail to the *U.S.S. North Carolina* for processing on September 8, 1919 probably because the other battleship was nearby and the post office on the *Oregon* had been discontinued three months earlier.

Very rare postmark showing hand-set type in words "BREMERTON" and "WASHINGTON" as part of the *U.S.S. Oregon* postmark on January 5, 1915. (Left) Round-dater used for REGISTERED mail handled in the postoffice on the *Oregon*.

Registered mail. The third style is the slotted 3-bar postmark where the postal clerk set in letters of the location of the ship when the stamp on the letter was cancelled. There are only six examples presently located.

Although this rubber stamp was merely used as a souvenir and had no postal purpose – there was no post office on the ship when it was berthed in Portland – it found its way onto this piece of undated mail.

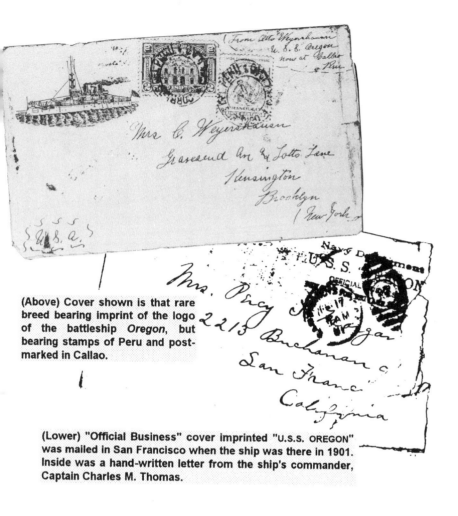

(Above) Cover shown is that rare breed bearing imprint of the logo of the battleship *Oregon*, but bearing stamps of Peru and postmarked in Callao.

(Lower) "Official Business" cover imprinted "U.S.S. OREGON" was mailed in San Francisco when the ship was there in 1901. Inside was a hand-written letter from the ship's commander, Captain Charles M. Thomas.

As mentioned, crew members often wrote letters on the ship, may have used the free covers provided by the ship for their letters, then mailed them in dock-side pouches or boxes. Postal Historians drool at the hope of finding such with a Punta Arenas, Chili, Rio de Janeiro, or Bahia, Brazil postmarks on the dates the *Oregon* visited. The letters would bear the stamps of those countries. Such a treasure has been found of an *Oregon* logo cover with stamp of Peru and postmark of Callao in 1899.

Persons who may stumble across postmarks of the battleship *Oregon* might wish to share sharp copies of them for possible inclusion in a future addition of this book. The publisher's address is on page iv. ✛

Appendix A.
Commanding Officers *USS Oregon*
1896 – 1919

(Records of the Department of the Navy Washington, D.C.)

Rank and Name	Dates
Capt. Henry L. Howison	July 15, 1896 to Mar. 20, 1897
Capt. Albert S. Barker	Mar. 20, 1897 to Jan. 17, 1898
Capt. Alexander McCormick	Jan. 17, 1898 to Mar. 17, 1898
Capt. Charles E. Clark	Mar. 17, 1898 to Aug. 6, 1898
Capt. Albert S. Barker	Aug. 6, 1898 to May 29, 1899
Capt. George F. F. Wilde	May 29, 1899 to Feb. 22, 1901
Capt. Francis W. Dickins	Feb. 22, 1901 to April 5, 1901
Lt. Commander Chas. A. Adams	Apr. 5, 1901 to Apr. 7, 1901
Capt. Charles M. Thomas	Apr. 7, 1901 to Feb. 10, 1902
Capt. Joseph Giles Eaton	Feb. 10, 1902 to Aug. 29, 1902
Capt. William T. Burwell	Aug. 29, 1902 to Aug. 27, 1904
Capt. John P. Merrell	Aug. 27, 1904 to Apr. 26, 1906
(Temporarily Out of Commission)	Apr. 27, 1906 to Apr. 25, 1911
Capt. Charles F. Pond	Aug. 26, 1911 to Mar. 25, 1912
Lt. Commander Chas. T. Owens	Mar. 25, 1912 to Apr. 13, 1912
Lt. (jg) William P. Beeler	Apr. 13, 1912 to Apr. 16, 1912
Lt. Edison E. Scranton	Apr. 16, 1912 to June 28, 1912
Lt. Comdr. Henry N. Jenson	June 28, 1912 to July 20, 1912
Lt. Comdr. James J. Raby	July 20, 1912 to July 24, 1912
Lt. Edison E. Scranton	July 24, 1912 to Aug. 2, 1913
Lt. Comdr. Henry N. Nelson	Aug. 2, 1913 to Aug. 14, 1913
Commander Charles J. Lang	Aug. 14, 1913 to Aug. 22, 1913
Lt. Comdr. Henry N. Jenson	Aug. 22, 1913 to Aug. 24, 1913
Lt. (jg) Frank R. King	Aug. 24, 1913 to Sept. 12, 1913
Lt. (jg) S. 0. Greig	Sep. 12, 1913 to Jan. 8, 1914
Lt. Comdr. Henry N. Jenson	Jan. 8, 1914 to Apr. 25, 1914
Lt. Comdr. M. St. C. Ellis	Apr. 25, 1914 to June 11, 1914
Lt. J. S. McCain	June 11, 1914 to July 28, 1914
Lt. Comdr. B. T. Bulmer	July 28, 1914 to Dec. 15, 1914
Lt. Comdr. Z. E. Briggs	Dec. 15, 1914 to Jan. 13, 1915
Commander J. M. Reeves	Jan. 13, 1915 to May 8, 1916
Commander G. W. Williams	May 8, 1916 to Apr. 23, 1917
Lt. Comdr. F. B. Freyer	Apr. 23, 1917 to Aug. 27, 1917
Commander C. P. Snyder	Aug. 27, 1917 to May 24, 1918
Commander A. B. Hoff	May 24, 1918 to Dec. 31, 1918
Lt. Comdr. W. E. Madden	Dec. 31, 1918 to Jan. 20, 1919
Capt. W. T. Tarrant	Jan. 20, 1919 to June 6, 1919
Lt. Comdr. A. G. Olson	Jun 6, 1919 to June 12, 1919
(Temporarily out of Commission)	Jun 13, 1919 to Aug. 20, 1919
Capt. I. C. Wettengill	Aug. 21, 1919 to Oct. 4, 1919
De-Commissioned	Oct. 4, 1919

Appendix B.
Naval and Marine Officers On Board
USS Oregon
During Battle of Santiago de Cuba

Captain Charles E. Clark; Commanding

Lt. Commander James K. Cogwell (Executive Officer); General charge of the batteries

Lt. Reginald F. Nicholson (Navigator); Placing the ship as directed

Lt. William H. Allen; In charge of the ammunition supplies

Lt. Albert A. Ackerman; In charge of after 13-inch turret

Lt. (jg) Edward W. Eberly; In charge of forward 13-inch turret

Lt. (jg) Clarence M. Stone; In charge of 6-inch battery

Ensign Lucius A. Bostwick; Aloft giving ranges until closed then torpedo officer

Ensign Charles L. Hussey; In charge of 10, 6-Pdr H. R. F. guns

Ensign Rufus Z. Johnston, Jr.(Signal Officer); In charge of signals and aide to captain

Captain of Marines Randolph Dickens; Commander of Marines and 4, 6-Pdr H.R.F. guns

2nd Lt. of Marines Austin R. Davis; In charge of 4, 6-Pdr H. R. F. Guns and 2, 1-Pdrs

Naval Cadet Harry E. Yarnell; In charge port after 8-inch turret

Naval Cadet Samuel G. Magill; In charge of 6-inch gun

Naval Cadet Clarence F. Kempff; In charge of after starboard 8-inch turret

Naval Cadet Paul B. Dugan; In forward 13-inch turret

Naval Cadet Everet J. Sadler; In charge of forward chain of supplies

Naval Cadet Edward C. Kalbfus; In after 13-inch turret

Naval Cadet Harry L. Brinser; In after chain of supplies

Naval Cadet Charles B. Hatch; At secondary battery.

Naval Cadet Chauncey R. Shackford; In torpedo division

Naval Cadet Overstreet; In charge of forward starboard 8-inch turret

Chief Engineer Robert W. Milligan; In charge of Engine Room

Passed Assistant Engineer Cleland N. Offley; In starboard Engine Room.

Assistant Engineer Joseph M. Reeves; In port Engine Room

Assistant Engineer Frank Lyon; In charge of fire rooms

Naval Cadet (engineer division) Henry N. Jenson; In after Hydraulic Pump Room

Naval Cadet (engineer division) William D. Leahy; In forward Hydraulic Pump Room

Assistant Engineer Thad C. Dunlap; In starboard Engine Room.

Surgeon Phillips A. Lovering (Medical Officer); In charge of ship's hospital

Assistant Surgeon Washington B. Grove; Transportation of wounded

Paymaster Samuel R. Calhoun; Assigned to Surgeon – aid to wounded

Chaplain Joseph P. McIntyre; With Surgeon – aid to wounded

Pay Clerk Joseph A. Murphy; Assigned to aid to wounded in 6-inch compartment

Boatswain John Costello; In central station

Gunner Arthur S. Williams; In Powder Division

Carpenter Milton F. Roberts; In Powder Division

As years passed, many of the junior officers and the Naval Cadets became prominent in
naval history.

Appendix C.
The Crew on Board
USS Oregon
During Battle of Santiago de Cuba

(The accuracy of this roster can not be guaranteed. –Editor)

Acors, Jacob, Landsman
Adams, Morris Nelson, Seaman
Affleck, Harry Watson, Machinist 2d class
Ahlim, Charles, Seaman
Allen, Harry, Apprentice 2d class
Allison, James, Gunner's Mate 3rd class (Actg.)
Almquist, Gustav Sigfrid, Seaman
Anderson, John, Sailmaker
Anderson, Clarence, Apprentice 2d class
Anderson, John, Seaman
Anderson, George William, Seaman
Annett, Charles Frank Jr., Ordinary seaman
Arnbros, Otto Joseph. Apprentice 2d class
Attridge, 'Peter, Coal Passer
Atwood, Charles Matthews, Seaman
Ausseresses, Paul Robert, Seaman
Auld, Richard, Landsman
Ausin, George Churchill, Landsman
Ayers, Archie, Coal Passer

Bagley, Frank Leslie, Apprentice 2d class
Beale, George, Fireman 2d class
Beazley, George Arthur, Apprentice 2d class
Bedwarsky, Louis, Boatswain 1st class
Beebe, John Kinney, Ordinary Seaman
Begley, Frank Bernard, Apprentice 2d class
Belknap, William Henry, Yeoman 1st class (Actg.)
Bensinger, Albert Nathan, Ordinary Seaman
Bengtsson, Johan August, Q-master 2d class (Actg.)
Berry, Arthur Edward, Apprentice 2d class
Blandenberg, Charles, Fireman 1st class
Blundell, William Henry, Fireman 1st class
Boning, Carl Hans Johanse, Machinist 2d class
Bouldron, William, Coal passer
Bourke, James, Fireman 1st Class
Boylan, Charles Wesley, Landsman
Bradley, William Alexander, Machinist 2nd class
Bradley, Alexander Stuart, Seaman
Brasor, Dennis Michael, Fireman 1st class

Broaden, Samuel Leo, Landsman
Brounty, Theodore, Landsman
Brown, Joe, Ordinary Seaman
Brown, William Ransford, Seaman
Burns, John Richard, Coal passer
Burns, Joseph Peter, Fireman 1st class
Burns, William, Gunner's mate 1st class
Burrows, John, Ordinary Seaman

Cademartori, John, Coxswain (Actg.)
Caldano, Emil, Seaman
Calori, Sebastian, Landsman
Careighton, John William, Landsman
Carlstrom, Carl Oskar, Seaman
Carlton, Frank, Blacksmith
Campbell, John Peter, Seaman
Casey, James, Coal passer
Chan, Duck, Mess attendant
Chace, Paul Griswold, Seaman
Chase, Walter Sargent, Gunner 3rd class (Actg.)
Christianson, Charles Jacob, Chief Yeoman
Christopher, Willis Adam, Seaman
Clark, Thomas, Water tender (Actg.)
Clute, Frank, Chief Yeoman
Close, Orin Samuel, Apprentice 2d class
Clynes, John William, Apprentice 2d class
Collins, Patrick Lawrence, Coal passer
Collins, Ward Oliver, Seaman
Content, Sherlie Shelby, Coal passer
Converse, Sullivan, Seaman
Crego, Flyod Louis, Apprentice 2d class
Creigbton, Frederick, Apprentice 2d class
Crosby, Frank, Gunner 3rd class (Actg.)
Culbertson, Frank Andrew, Coal passer
Cuneo, Rinaldo, Seaman
Cunningham William Arthur, Coal passer
Curry, Daniel, Coal passer
Curtin, William Husted, Coxswain (Actg.)
Cummings, William Edward, Landsman

Cullinan, Stanley Baldwin, Ordinary seaman
Grosman, Earl, Ordinary seaman

Danford, Roydon R., Apprentice 1st class
Davenport Mateland A., Landsman
Davis, Charles, Coxswain (Actg.)
Davis, Guy Alonzo, Landsman
Davis, Harry, Apprentice 2d class
Davis, John, Seaman
Davis, William Clarence, Seaman
Dell, William John, Landsman
Dennison, Charles Robert, Seaman
Dieudonne, Eugene James, Coal passer
Dillon, John James, Water tender (Actg.)
Ding, Ah, Mess attendant
Ditson, John George, Oiler (Actg.)
Doherty, Philip, Chief Gunner's Mate
Donahue, Edward, Water tender (Actg.)
Donahue, Joseph Patrick, Coal passer
Doud, Wilhard Orrin, Ordinary seaman
Douglas, Robert John Jr., Ordinary seaman
Dresser, William, Fireman 1st class
Drewery, Lorenzo Willows, Coal passer
Drummond, Arthur William, Machinist 2d class
Driscoll, Edward, Ordinary seaman
Driscoll, John Charles, Apprentice 2d class
Doherty, George, Seaman
Dugan, Robert E., Apprentice 2d class
Duncan, John, Ordinary seaman
Duff, Roden Robinson, Seaman
Dunne, James, Fireman 2d class
Dunning, Charles M., Ordinary seaman
Dyer, Spencer Howard, Apprentice 3rd class

Easterbrook, James, Chief gunner's mate
Eberling, Fred Theodore, Landsman
Edwards, Bertram Willard, Ordinary seaman
Edwards, John Timothy, Gunner 2nd class (Actg.)
Ellis, John, Seaman
English, John Joseph, Ordinary seaman
Evans, Thomas, Water tender

Faulkner, Jacob Zigler, Ordinary seaman
Felsher, John, Boatswain 1st class (Actg.)
Fennessy, Patrick, Landsman
Ferguson, William Earnest, Apprentice 2d class
Fetter, Harry, Landsman

Fitzgerald, John Howard, Seaman
Fokken, John Henry Gerard. Seaman
Flater, James, Coxswain (Actg.)
Floyd, William Lee, Landsman
Fluhart, Waylend Edward, Yeoman 2nd class (Actg.)
Flynn, James Francis, Fireman 2d class
Franks, George Worga, Seaman
Frederickson, Hans, Oiler (Actg.)
Frederickson, John, Fireman 1st class
French, Arthur Boynton, Fireman 2d class
Fry, Karl, Seaman
Foley, John Charles, Apprentice 2d class
Furlong, Thomas Francis, Seaman

Gage, Benjamin Franklin, Seaman
Gallagher, Patrick James, Fireman 1st class
Galvin, John, Ship's cook 4th class
Ganeau, Edward, Landsman
Gannon, Joseph Cuthbert, Seaman
Gartley, Alonzo, Apprentice 2d class
Gavin, Edward Joseph, Gunner 1st class
Gertsen, Andrew, Coxswain (Actg.)
Gibbons, Martin Francis, Machinist 2nd class
Giles, Harry Marshall
Gill, Adam, Coal passer
Ginzl, Joseph, Coal passer
Glazier, William Alexander, Fireman 1st class
Goddard, William Henry, Seaman
Goldsmith, Joseph
Gong, Ah, Wardroom steward
Good, Walter A., Landsman
Goodnow, Joseph Victor, Apprentice 2d class
Grady, John Patrick
Grant, James, Fireman 1st class
Gratz, Edward, Chief master-at-arms
Gray, John, Seaman
Gray, Thomas, Coal passer
Green, Benjamin James, Coxswain (Actg.)
Greenwood, Harry A., Ordinary seaman
Green, Douglas Barton, Ordinary seaman
Greenwood, John, Ordinary seaman
Grigg, Edward Charles, Coal passer
Groves, James Francis, Gunner 1st class
Gulkich, Milan, Apprentice 2d class
Gustavson, Ernest Alexis, Gunner 3rd class

Hafke, Charles Frederick P., Seaman

Halberg, Hjalmar William, Seaman
Hall, John, Fireman 3rd class
Hamilton, Robert, Seaman
Hamlin, Joseph Wilfred, Seaman
Hanafin, Asher Alvin, Fireman 2d class
Hanafin, Albert Turnar, Fireman 1st class
Hansen, Lauritz, Boatswain 2d class
Hansen, Christ L. Coal passer
Harden, Clarence Gardener, Seaman
Harris, Willie Edward, Apprentice 2d class
Hartineyer, Andrew, Blacksmith
Harding, Michael, Seaman
Harman, George, Seaman
Hart, Frederick, Apprentice 2d class
Hassig, George, Coal passer
Havlik-, James, Seaman
Hayden, Charles Henery, Landsman
Hayden, John Bruce, Coal passer
Heiberger, William, Coppersmith (Actg.)
Hellman, Johan Alexander, Seaman
Hello, Johnnes, Machinist 1st class
Hewel, Clarence, Apprentice 3rd class
Heye, Robert, Apprentice 2d class
Hickey, William James, Gunner 3rd class (Actg.)
High, Lester Valentine, Landsman
Hill, James Edward, Ordinary seaman
Hille, Martin, Coal passer
Hirokawa, Tsu, Steerage steward
Hogart, James Isaac, Fireman 2d class
Hostrup, Christian, Ordinary seaman
Huber, Mick O., Acting chief yeoman
Hunter, Arthur Clair, Coal passer
Hyde, Charles James, (rate not stated)
Ichinose, Shircichi, Mess attendant
Ingalls, Robert M., Seaman

Jackson, William, Seaman
Jarvis, Edwin, Shipwright
Jock, Ah, Mess attendant
Joehnk, Henry Edward, Apprentice 2d class
Johns, Henry Carl, Seaman
Johnson, Charles, Seaman
Johnson, Gustav, Chief Gunner
Johnson, Otto, Chief machinist
Jones, Robert, Coal passer
Jonsen, Andrew, Gunner 2d class

Jonssen, Hjalmer, Gunner 3rd class

Kamiya, Takematsu, Cabin cook
Keller, Joseph Anton, Seaman
Kehke, Michael, Coxswain (Actg.)
Kennedy, John, Landsman
Keough, William Michael, Gunner 2d class
King, George Alexander, Seaman
King, John Wilson, Apprentice 2d class
Klingel, Chester Clark, Landsman
Knight, Frank, Fireman 1st class

Lake, Charles Edward, Quartermaster 1st class
Lamb, Wilfred Owen, Gunner 1st class
Langevin, Albert, Oiler (Actg.)
Lanzing, Charles, Gunner 1st class
Larsen, Ole, Coxswain (Actg.)
Larson, Albin Oscar, Gunner 1st class
Laughton, Raymond Marion, Landsman
Lawrence, Herbert Franklin, Coal passer
Leasure, Edward Anthony, Gunner 1st class
Lee, Theodore Augustine, Landsman
Leffingwell, Ernest DeKoven, Seaman
Leighton, Ellington, Boatswain 1st class
Lemon, Thomas Benton, Seaman
Lewis, Frank, Coal passer
Lewis, John Douglas, Apprentice 2nd class
Lewis, Frank, Water tender
Lindstrom, William, Gunner 3rd class (Actg.)
Long, Clarence Albert, Seaman
Lockwood, Travis Drake, Bayman
Love, George Christopher, Apprentice 2nd class
Loy, Chang, Mess attendant
Lubeck, Erick M., Seaman
Lucey, John, Ordinary seaman
Lundin, Charles, Seaman
Lung, Ah, Wardroom cook
Lyon, James Sedgley, Apprentice 2nd class
Lyon, William, Fireman 1st class
Lyons, James, Fireman 1st class

Madson, Carl John,. Gunner 2d class (Actg.)
Martin, Edward, Landsman
Marue, Harry, Warrant Officer's cook
Masutani, Toyotaro, Warrant Officer's steward
Matthews, Walter, Ordinary seaman
Mell, Frederick, Apprentice 2d class

Mengula, Antonio Michel, Apprentice 2d class
Meredith, Floyd Eaty, Seaman
Merritt, Arthur, Ordinary seaman
Middleton, Walter Thomas, Apprentice 2d class
Miller, Fritz, Seaman
Miller, Otto, Painter
Miner, Thomas Edward, Landsman
Mitchell, Harry Moxley, Apprentice 1st class
Michell, William John, Apprentice 2d class
Morean, John, Oiler
Morris, Wilham Louis, Seaman
Morrison, James Henery, Chief machinist
Moss, James, Machinist 1st class
Moss, Bernard, Fireman 1st class
Mullins, Thomas, Seaman
Murray, Samuel, Fireman 2d class
Munz, Joseph Gustav. Fireman 2d class
Murray, George Washington, Landsman
Murphey, Edward James, Seaman
Murphy, Daniel Joseph, Fireman 2d class
Murphy, Stanislaus Joseph, Seaman
Murphy, James Henry, Coxswain (Actg.)
Murphy, John, Chief Boatswain (Actg.)
Murphy, John, Machinist 1st class (Actg.)
Murphy, Melvin Benjamin, Coal passer
Moore, Benjamin Butler, Plumber and fitter
Moore, Charles John, Ordinary seaman
Montgomery, Arthur Smith, Fireman 1st class

MacKnight, William George, Apprentice 2d class
McCarthey, Eugene, Chief machinist (Actg.)
McDowell, Edgar, Coal passer
McEwen, Samuel Horace, Seaman
McGarigal, James, Fireman 1st class
McGuire, John James, Apprentice 1st class
McHugh, William Henry, Seaman
McKachney, Thomas, Boatswain 2d class
McKeon, Owen Peter, Coal passer
McKinney, Allen Barrett, Ordinary seaman
McNaught, William, Fireman 2d class
McQuarrie, Murdock James, Coal passer
McVay, Joseph Alphonses, Machinist 2d class

Nagata, Shirogiro, Mess attendant
Nagelstock, Edwin Harry, Seaman
Nelson, Frederick J., Landsman
Neuman, Adolph, Coal passer

Newman, Philip, Seaman
Nicholson, Robert, Boatswain 1st class
Nickell, George Guy, Coal passer
Nickerson, Edgar Francis, Landsman
Nilson ' Charles Alfred, Seaman
Nord, Johan Erikson, Seaman
Norman, John, Seaman
Norris, William Henery, Boatswain 2nd class
Nylund, George, Boatswain 2d class

O'Brien, Joseph, Fireman 1st class
O'Connel, Andrew, Landsman
O'Neill, Thomas, Seaman
Oishi, Kitchitaro, Mess attendant
Olson, John, Carpenter 1st class
Omatsu, Ginjiro, Mess attendant
Oswald, Harold, Gunner 3rd class
Orton, James Edward, Apprentice 1st class
Ozard, William, Coal passer

Page, Cecil, Seaman
Pallo, Adam, Seaman
Patterson, John August, Gunner 3rd class
Pearman, William E., Apothecary
Peiper, August Otto, Shipwright
Perkins, Isom E., Coal passer
Peters, William Charles, Ordinary seaman
Peters, Frank, Seaman
Pierce, William Henry, Apprentice 2d class
Pilgrim, William, Apprentice 2d class
Pope, Benjamin, Seaman
Powell, Scyron Hugh, Coal passer
Powers, George Daniel, Apprentice 2d class
Power, Thomas Michael, Carpenter 3rd class
Priddy, Albert, Coal passer

Quinn, James Arthur, Apprentice 2d class

Randolph, Robert, Ordinary seaman
Rea, John Henry, Landsman
Regley, Joseph, Landsman
Reitz, John, Seaman
Richardson, Ray Wess, Landsman
Rigo, Frank, Seaman
Riley, Francis Bennett, Seaman
Roberts, Edward Owen, Machinist 2d class
Roberts, Thomas John, Seaman
Robinson, Charles Frank, Apprentice 2d class

Robinson, George W., Fireman 2d class
Robinson, William Ford, Landsman
Robertson, Marion, Fireman 1st class
Rose, Frank, Fireman 2d class
Rose, Joseph Raymond, Apprentice 2d class
Rosen, Emanuel, Apprentice 2d class
Ross Guy Austin, Fireman 2d class
Ross, John Joseph, Plumber and fitter (Actg.)
Roy James M., Seaman

Sanderson, George, Seaman
Sands, George Washington, Coal passer
Saracco, Joseph M., Apprentice 2d class
Saxai, Kenekich, Steerage cook
Scadden, Charles David, Apprentice 2d class
Schildhauer, Jacob Frederick, Coal passer
Schlicht, George, Apprentice 2d class
Schroder, Julius Frederick, C., Fireman 2d class
Schultz, Paul Horatio, Machinist 2d class
Schweizer, George Godfrey, Landsman
Schultz, Gustav Axel Henrich, Seaman
Scott, Edward, Oiler (Actg.)
Shantz, Joseph Edward, Seaman
Shaw, Calvin Adelbert, Apprentice 2d class
Shaw, John Martin Andrew, Master-at-arms 1st class
Shilling, George, Master-at-arms 2d class (Actg.)
Shinick, John Joseph, Coal passer
Sidall, Joseph James, Seaman
Sieberman, Frank, Bayman
Slade James, Seaman
Sloan, William Grimes, Apprentice 2d class
Small, Robert H., Chief machinist
Smith, Edward, Oiler (Actg.)
Smith, Frank, Coal passer
Smith, John Henery, Coal passer
Smith, Samuel Herbert, Machinist 1st class (Actg.)
Smith, Thomas Jefferson, Boilermaker
Smith, Wedster Temple, Seaman
Smith, William, Gunner 3rd class
Southard, Francis Charles, Seaman
Sowerby, Wilham Doberty, Ship's cook 1st class
Spivey, Charles B., Gunner 1st class (Actg.)
Sparks, Frederick Grover, Apprentice 2d class
Spooner, Walter Frederick, Apprentice 2d class
Sporner, Reed E., Coal passer
Sprague, Leroy Augustus, Apprentice 2d class

Spratt, Thomas Atkinson, Apprentice 1st class
Squire, Paul Edwin, Bayman
Stanley, Sewin, Quartermaster 3rd class (Actg.)
Stein, Abraham, Apprentice 2d class
Stephens, Charles Frawley, Coal passer
Sterrit, Everit Charles, Fireman 1st class
Stetson, Frank Charlie, Coal passer
Stevens, Charles Edward, Seaman
Steward, William, Oiler (Actg.)
Stricker, Edward, Apprentice 2d class
Stuckey, William John, Ordinary seaman
Sugenoya, Shinobu, Mess attendant
Sullivan, Joseph Francis, Master-at-arms 2d class (Actg.)
Summers, Frank, Water tender (Actg.)
Sutton, James, Seaman
Swanson, John Peter, Seaman
Sweeney, Gabriel A., Apprentice 2d class

Tanaka, Henry, Mess attendant
Taschek, Max, Oiler (Actg.)
Thirmes, Peter, Coxswain
Thomas, Frank Cole Veliz, David E.
Thompson, William A., Seaman
Tildermann, Carl Frederick, Seaman
Tillett, James Clarence, Seaman
Tong, Wong, Mess attendant
Townsend, John, Foreman 2d class
Tracey, Thomas, Oiler (Actg.)
Trego, Davit, Coxswain (Actg.)
Tulley, Peter Samuel, Fireman 1st class
Tulloch, Gilbert, Seaman

Vahlbusch, George Herman, Apprentice 2d class
Veliz, David E., Bugler

Wall, George Ignacicus F., Apprentice 2d class
Walker, Joseph Frederick, Landsman
Wardwell, Charles A., Chief machinist
Watson, Edgar Francis, Seaman
Wedin, Edward I., Ordinary seaman
Wharton, Joseph William, Apprentice 2d class
White, Robert William, Seaman
Whisker, Frank Colter, Apprentice 2d class
William, Henry, Gunner 3rd class (Actg.)
Williams, Charles Hughbert, Apprentice 2d class
Willis, Samuel, Fireman 1st class
Wilson, William, Landsman

Wing, Chon, Mess attendant
Wollensak, Florian D., Ordinary seaman
Wood, Benjamin Bechenough, Apprentice 2d class
Wood, Joel Benjamin, Ordinary seaman
Wright, Thomas Boyer, Apprentice 2d class

Yeigh, Clarence Leslie, Ordinary seaman
Yung, Jee, Mess attendant

Zelinsky, Abraham Adolph, Painter (Actg.)

Appendix D.
United States Marines on Board
Battleship *Oregon*
During Battle of Santiago de Cuba

(Although edited to May 21, 1998, accuracy of this list can not be guaranteed. –Editor)

Captain Randolph Dickins
2nd Lt. Austin R. Davis
1st Sgt. Henry F. Bray
Sgt. Frederick A. Ramsey
Sgt. George Heiligenstein
Sgt. John C. Hunter
Corp. William Delaney
Corp. Thomas J. Howlett
Corp. Edgar B. Work
Corp. George Doss
Corp. William J. Boyd
Drummer William Ebert
Fifer Albert M. Colson
Private John H. Allen
Private James Ayling
Private Erwin J. Boydston
Private John P. Benrenhafer
Private John Butts
Private Delbert L. Chaffee
Private Robert Cross
Private James M. Curtis
Private John P. Donovan
Private Alek Herskind
Private Albert Moore
Private Charles Miller
Private Comelius Moynahan
Private Martin L. M. Mueller
Private Chris. C. Mullen
Private Joseph H. O'Shea (Fired first gun at Battle of Santiago de Cuba)
Private Carl A. Peterson
Private Evan Prechard
Private Frank Rose
Private David J. Scannell
Private Albert L. Sewell
Private Frank B. Slaght

**Sampson Medal
Navy and Marine Corps**
Awarded to officers and
men of the Navy and Marine
Corps who participated in the
engagements in the West Indies.

Private Denis E. Smith
Private James A. Sullvan
Private Robert E. Thomas
Private Joseph Truehaft
Private Albert Turner

Private Oscar J. Upham
Private William A. Waters
Private Charles Wilson

TRANSFERRED:
Private Charles E. Keating
Private John Leahy

Appendix E
Commendation by the
Bureau of Steam Engineering

Engineer-in-Chief George W. Melville. USN, Chief of the Bureau of Steam Engineering in his annual report of 1898, commented on the *Oregon's* achievement:

It has not been customary to call special attention to the performance of vessels except on trials under maximum conditions, but that of the *Oregon* is so exceptional that it deserves a record in the Bureau's report. She was ordered from the Pacific to the Gulf before war was declared, and leaving Puget Sound 6 March, arrived at Jupiter Inlet 24 May, having steamed over 14,500 miles, stopping only for coal, and not being delayed an hour anywhere through any derangements of the machinery. Stopping at Key West only long enough to coal, she took her place in the blockading fleet at Sartiago, and was always ready for service.

This alone would have given her an unparalleled record among battleships but the culmination came in the great battle of 3 July, when she surpassed herself. Always ready for action, she speedily attained a power greater than that developed on the trial, giving a speed (on account of greater displacement and foul bottom) only slightly less than then attained, and distancing all the other ships except the *Brooklyn*, which is 5 knots faster. Every official report comments on her wonderful speed, and it is generally believed that but for it, one at least, and possibly two, of the Spanish ships might have escaped.

The whole record is thus one which has never been equaled in the history of navies, and it will remain the standard for a long time to come. The credit is due, in the first place, to the builders – the Union Iron Works – for the excellence of the material ard workmarship, but still more, and chiefly, to the engineering department of the vessel. The Bureau, therefore, takes great pleasure in commending to the Department's most favorable consideration Chief Engineer Robert W. Milligan, the executive head of the department, for his professional ability, untiring care and <u>excellent</u> discipline; and also the junior engineer officers and the enlisted men, whose faithfulness and zeal, under most trying circumstances, have enabled our Navy to add this to the other brilliant records of our vessels. ✛

130

Appendix F
Biographical Sketch of
Rear Admiral Charles E. Smith
Commander, *USS Oregon,* Battle of Santiago de Cuba

"That Clark boy will make a mark for himself yet" the old timers would say of Charles Edgar Clark who was born August 10, 1843, at Bradford, Vermont. His parents were not wealthy and he had to work hard for whatever he wanted. He was remembered by old residents as having the ideals of older heads rather than those of a boy: He had one brother older than he who went west and settled in Michigan.

Clark was an imaginative youngster and while not lacking in courage to meet the ordinary demands – give and take of his boyish world – his head was pretty well full with the idea of fanciful dangers. Preeminent among them were a fearful trio: Abductors, barn-burners, and ghosts.

He was particularly fond of history and read everything he could lay his hands on concerning Hannibal, Napoleon, Marlborough and other great generals.

He received an appointment to the United States Naval Academy at Annapolis for the class of 1864. The historic frigate *Constitution* "Old Ironsides" had just been fitted out as a schoolship. He went aboard.

At the opening of the Civil War, many changes came to the Academy. The boys from the south resigned. The northern boys were placed on the *Constitution* which was made ready for war. Its class room had gone and the guns had been shifted from the spar deck.

Clark saw the open sea for the first time from the deck of "Old Ironsides." Strange that two great ships should play a part, one in the first of his career and the other, the battleship *Oregon* near the last. But today, only the *Constitution* and the *Olympia,* from the Battle of Manila Bay, remain.

Young Clark served with distinction during the Civil War

under Farragut and Porter on the Mississippi River.

After the Civil War he rose rapidly in rank. At the age of twenty-four, in 1868, he passed the examination for Lieutenant-Commander. He served on different ships both on the Atlantic and the Pacific Coasts and was promoted to Captain in 1896 and given command of the *Monterey* at San Diego, California. He was still in command of the *Monterey* in 1898 when orders came for him to proceed to San Francisco and take command of the battle-ship *Oregon*.

The *Oregon* left San Francisco Bay on March 19, 1898 with sealed orders. He proceeded through the Golden Gate and headed South. Brief stops were made along the way for coaling and a few adjustments as his ship was still new. Captain Clark kept in close contact with his officers and man and did everything to keep them contented and happy. The men appreciated their commander's consideration and in turn were ready and willing to give their best to him at any time.

Just thirty-two years before, Captain Clark had passed through the Straits of Magellan on the consort of the *Monadnock,* the first armored ship to round South America. Now he was commander of the second iron-clad ship to make the passage. But this time he was hurrying in the opposite direction to strengthen the navy on the Atlantic Coast.

Many are the trials to be surmounted in a voyage of any vessel but to a battleship making such an unprecedented trip, there was something new to be reckoned with every minute.

Captain Clark, with firm determination accepted the challenges of the forced-draft transit of the Strait and finally entered the Atlantic Ocean. With stops along the South American coast for coal, he arrived at Key West on May 26. Two days later, the *Oregon* became a part of Admiral Watson's fleet then left on the 700 mile voyage to join the blockade at the entrance of the harbor of Santiago, Cuba.

After long days and nights of waiting, the enemy came forth from the harbor. In what later seemed to have been only a matter of minutes, under Captain Clark's command, additional history was made by the battleship *Oregon*.

Following the long, stressful voyage of the sea-run from San

Francisco, then the naval engagement off Santiago, Captain Clark was hospitalized to rest.

He was appointed Rear Admiral and filled many responsible posts. The last, from 1901 to 1904, he was Governor of the Naval Home in Philadelphia. Later he was billeted in Washington as President of Examining and Retirement Boards. He retired August 10, 1905.

*   *   *

Charles E. Clark married Marie Louise Davis, on April 8, 1869 in Greenfield, Massachusetts. The bride was the daughter of Wendel T. David of Greenfield. Two daughters were born to them who kept the tradition of the Navy by each marrying graduates of the U. S. Naval Academy class of 1886. Mary Louise Clark married S. S. Robinson, who became a Rear Admiral and Caroline Russell Clark became the wife of Rear Admiral C. F. Hughes.

After his retirement on August 10, 1905 Rear Admiral Clark renewed his old love of history and traveled considerably abroad. He first spend nearly one year in the European Countries bordering the Mediterranean Sea with much time in Greece where he became an authority on its history.

After his return from Europe, he lived on the Pacific Coast at Bremerton, home of the Puget Sound Navy Yard and at Santa Barbara. Most of his later life was spent in New England until a year before his death when he again visited California.

Rear Admiral Charles E. Clark died at the home of his daughter in Long Beach, California on October 1, 1922. He was 79. His body was transported to Arlington National Cemetery where he was buried with full military honors. ✢

Appendix G.
Affect of the Washington Naval Conference on Limitations of Weapons on the Battleship *Oregon*

The terms of the Five Power Naval Limitation Treaty signed by Britain, France, Italy, Japan and the United States, frequently called the Washington Naval Treaty of 1922, detailed restrictions on tonnages of warships over 10,000 tons displacement. The treaty allowed 5 ships to Britain and 5 ships to the U.S., 3 for Japan and 1.67 each for France and Italy in addition to other provisions not related to numbers or tonnages of ships.

Nations that had more ships than the treaty allowed were to destroy the excess. The battleship *Oregon,* 10,228 tons, was over the weight limit and it was obsolete thus was ordered disarmed and destroyed. But the ship was revered by Americans as a priceless, historic relic and to break it up was unthinkable. By a resolution of Congress and an order from the Secretary of the Navy, the ship was purposefully put out of commission to comply with the treaty but spared the shipbreakers mall. It was instead, prepared as a floating monument.

Rendering the *Oregon* inoperable included removing the engines; sections were cut from cylinders by acetylene torch and the main drive shafts were severed. The big guns were made non-firable by drilling holes in them and in their operating mechanisms. Her former commander, Captain R. T. Menner, USN, declared the ship to be totally inoperable. Further, he said it would be less costly to build a new modern battleship than to repair the old one.

To the public appearance, however, the battleship *Oregon* looked fine because the Puget Sound Navy Yard had repainted the vessel inside and out. The furniture had been restored. The ship was delivered by tug boats to Portland, Oregon as completely as possible for the pupose of looking good as a memorial museum piece as well as to the Navy which still owned it. ✛

About the Author

Although unaware of it at the time, notes from Bert Webber's interview with Colonel Andrew S. Rowan (USA retired), for a school journalism class project in 1937, would eventually be included in the present work. Webber grew up in San Francisco. The Presidio of San Francisco, where the Colonel lived in retirement at Letterman General Hospital, was familiar to him.

Webber entered the Regular United States Army within a few months of his 1940 high school graduation. He went directly into the Signal Corps because in high school, electric shop and journalism were his two better subjects. His Army life includes duty in Alaska where he landed with a cadre of Signal men six months before the start of WWII. While there in telephone work, he also worked as a Signal Corps Photographer. He later went into pilot training with the Air Force but when be was invited to go back to the Signal Corps for newsreel camera work, be promptly hung up his flying togs.

He later served in Scotland, England, Belgium and France.

In the post-war world, for a decade he owned and operated a commercial photographic business and camera shop at Sedro-Woolley, Washington. He also wrote for the Seattle *Post-Intelligencer* and later for the *Oregon Journal.* Following a stint sell-ing Remington office machines, he was admitted to Whitworth College as a journalism major. He later earned the Master of Library Science degree at the University of Portland.

His work as a school librarian in Lake Oswego and Medford, Oregon was rewarding but never satisfying so he retired in 1970 to do full time writing. Since 1970, Bert Webber has written many dozens of feature articles, particularly for the *Oregon Journal,* as well as over 60 books. His books, all non-fiction, are primarily about Oregon, the Oregon Trail and World War II.

While most of today's readers are unaware of it other than from Webber's books, in WWII the Japanese were bombing and killing people in the United States. His *magnum opus* is his internationally acclaimed work about these mysterious attacks all of which are documented in *Silent Siege-III; Japanese Attacks on North America in World War II, Ships Sunk, Air Raids, Bombs Dropped, Civilians Killed.* A second book deals with the Japanese having seized part of Alaska. Webber documents this in *Aleutian Headache, Deadly WWII Battles Fought on American Soil.*

Bert Webber is listed in *Contemporary Authors* and in *Who's Who in the West* and in *Who's Who in America.*

He and his wife Margie, who has co-authored a number of books with him, have four children and eight grand children. The Webber's live in Oregon's Rogue River Valley. ✢

Bibliography

Alden, Cdr. John D. USN. "Whatever Happened to the Battleship *Oregon?* in *Proceedings*. U.S. Naval Institute. Vol. 94. No. 9. pp. 146-149.

Aaron, Louise. "Old Oregon To See Active War Service" in *Oregon Journal*. Apr. 15, 1944. p.1.

Clark, Charles E. *My Fifty Years in the Navy*. Little, Brown. 1917.

"The Battleship Oregon" in *Congressional Record – House*. May 27, 1935 V.79 : 109 pp. 8559-8561.

Dana, Marshall N. "Governor Sprague Gave Ship Despite Protests" in *Oregon Journal*. Apr. 15, 1944. (*See also:* entry for "Governor Sprague is reported")

Ellis, Edward S. *Ellis's History of the United States*. Western Book Syn. 1899.

Falk, Edwin A. *From Perry to Pearl Harbor*. Doubleday. 1943.

"Fire on the Oregon, Big Battleship Has Narrow Escape; Caused By Spontaneous Combustion" in *Morning Oregonian* Nov. 23, 1897.

Gannon, Joseph C. *The U.S.S. Oregon and the Battle of Santiago*. Comet. 1958.

"Governor Sprague is reported..." in *Oregon Voter*. Vol. 104, No. 17. p. 29. Apr. 22, 1944.

Graves, William Sidney. *America's Siberian Adventure, 1918-1920*. Cape & Smith. 1931.

Heiser, Victor G. (M.D.). *An American Doctor's Odyssey*. Norton. 1936.

Hemment, John C. *Cannon and Camera; Sea and Land Battles of the Spanish-American War in Cuba, Camp Lee, and the Return of the Soldiers*. Appleton. 1899.

Hartsook, Key. "Old Oregon Sails Again; Nears Final Berth" in *Oregon Journal*. Sept. 12, 1938. pp 1, 3.

Kemp. Peter, *The Oxford Companion to Ships & the Sea*. Oxford Univ. Pr. 1976.

Link, Arthur S. *The Papers of Woodrow Wilson*. Vol. 63 Sep 4 - Nov 5, 1919. Princeton Univ Pr. 1990.

Mahar, Ted. "Remembering the Glory Days of a True War Hero" in *Oregonian*. Oct. 24, 1993 p. B-1.

———. "*USS Oregon*: Battleship Was the First of the New U.S. Navy" in *Oregonian*. Oct. 24, 1993 p. B-7.

———. "Ceremony to Recall Launching" in *Oregonian*. Oct. 24, 1993 p. B-7.

Morison, Samuel E. *History of United States Naval Operations in World War II*. Little, Brown. Vol. II 1964. Vol. XV. 1962.

"Not the End of It, There Will Be Inquiry, Captrain Wilde's Report ... How the Vessel Struck," in *Oregonian* Sept. 4, 1900.

O'Toole, G. J. A. *Spanish War – An American Epic*. Norton. 1984.

Reynolds, Francis J. *The United States Navy From the Revolution to Date*. F. P. Collier. 1917.

Perles, Anthony. *The People's Railway; The History of the Municipal Railway of San Francsico*. Interurban Press. 1981.

Richards, Leverett. "U. S. Invasion of Siberia...." in *Oregonian*. Dec. 8, 1968 p. F-11.

Rickover, Adm. H[yman] G. Rickover. *How the Battleship* Maine *Was Destroyed*. Dept. of the Navy. [doc.] U.S. Gov Print O. 1976.

The Story of Our Wonderful Victories Told By Dewey, Schley, Wheeler and Other Heroes; A True Story of Our War With Spain By the Officers and Men of Our Army and Navy. American Book and Bible House (Phila.). n.d.

Scott, John D. "They Saw The Hulk of the Old Oregon" in *Oregon Journal* [Pacific Parade section] Oct. 14, 1945. p.3.

Stevens, Willard H. "The Battleship Oregon" in *The Veteran*. Vol. 20. No. 4. April 1937. p.11.

Swanberg, W. A. *Citizen Hearst*. Chas. Scribner's. 1961.

Tichenor, Mary Walker. *Dedicated to the Memory of All of the Boys Who Sailed "The Seven Seas" on ... The Battleship Oregon; The Bull Dog of the Navy*. Private print. 1942.

U.S.S. Oregon (No. 3); A Summary of its History. Bureau of Nav. U.S.N. nd.

Watterson, Henry. *History of the Spanish-American War*. Kuhlman. 1898.

Wilson, Edith Bolling. *My Memoir*. Bobbs-Merrill. 1938.

Illustration Credits

Cover Robert R. Strodel collection
ii   U.S.Naval Institute (USNI)
vi   USNI
7   (top) Bert Webber (BW); (Lower-left) BW; (Lower-right) Bert Webber collection (BWc)
8   BWc
14   BWc
16   BWc
19   BWc
20   BW
22   USNI
24   USNI
25   BW
27   USNI
28   Univ of Portland collection
29   BWc
32-33 BW
35   USNI
42-43 BWc
45-46 USNI
48   BW
50-52 BWc
53   (Left) USNI; (Right), BWc
55   BWc
56-57 USNI
60   Bwc
66   (Top) USNI; (Lower) City of Portland Archives (CPA)
68   USNI
70   (Top) USNI; (lower) BW
71-72 Hiroshima Pref. Public Library
75-76 USNI
79   USNI
80   Bwc
82   Sam Foster
83-84 USNI
85   John S. King Collection
92   USNI
95   BWc
96   CPA
97   (Top) CPA; (Lower) BWc
99   Bwc
100 BW
101 USNI
102 BW
103 BW
104 (Top) Dale Webber; (Lower) BW
105-107 BW
108 BWc
112 USNI
113 BWc
115 BWc
116 BWc
117 Universal Ship Cancellation Soc. (USCS)
118 BWc
119 (Top) Leonard Lukens collection; (Lower) James P. Myerson collection (JPMc);
120 (Top) JPMc; (Center) USCS; (Lower) BWc
121 (Top) JPMc; (Lower) Rob't R. Strodel collection
135 Margie Webber

Index

Illustrations, including maps, are indicated in **bold *italic*** type.
Spanish ships are designated "Sp."
Only major incidents about the *USS Oregon* are indexed

Adams, LtCdr. Charles A., 74
Ainsworth, Capt. J. C., 18
Ainsworth, Daisy, 18
Allard, Dean. 11, 12
Almirante Oquendo Sp. cruiser, *see:*
   Oquendo
American Siberian Expeditionary Force, 86ı
Anita (dispatch boat), 58
Apra Harbor, 111, 112, 113
Arlington Nat'l Cemetery. 133
armament, 21, *22*; 13" guns, *46;* Sp. *50*
Asahi Evening News (newspaper), *116*
Astoria, Ore., 78, *81*
Atlantic Eastern Raiding Sqdn., 57n

BB-3 (designation), 89, 109
Bahama Isls, 40
Bahia, Brazil, 38, 41, 64, 121; (map) *32*
Baja, Calif., 23
band (music), 54, *55*
Barbados Isl., 39, 41, 59; (map), *32*
Barker, Capt. Albert S., 23, 57, 67
Barker, Iva, 18
Battleship *Oregon* Memorial Marine Park,
   101, 102, 103, 105
Battle of Santiago de Cuba (chronology) 62
battleships (Jpnse), 71n, 73
Beeshler, Lt(jg). Wm. H., 78
Bethlehem Iron Works, 18
Billeter, Anne, 11
bow-crest (shield), *100, 101, 102, 104, 105*
Boxer (Rebellion), 71
Braun, Carl E., (W7HRV) 108
Bremerton, dry dock, *79; see also:* Puget
   Sound Navy Yard
British Columbia, 25
Broadway Bridge (Portland) 25
Brooklyn (cruiser), 41, *42*, 45, 49, 51, 52,
   53-54, 57, 60, 61, 87, 99
Brooklyn Navy yard, 63, *68*
Burnside Bridge (Portland) 94

Cabros Isl., 114
Cactus (USCG), 7
Cape St. Roque, 38, 39
Captain Clark presentation sword, 84
Cardiff coal, *see:* coal
casualties, in Guam, 114; in Sp-Am War, 58
Callao, Peru, 7, 30, 31, 33, 41, 64, 121;
   (map), *32*

cage mast, 77
capstan, *66*
Celtic (stores ship), 63
Cervera, Adm. Pascual C. Topete, 15, 37, 39,
   49, 59, 61
Chamoros (on Guam), *113*
Chogoku (newspaper), *71, 72*
Clark, Capt. Charles E., *8*, 26, *53*, 54, 57, 59,
   61; died, 133
coal, (Cardiff), 52, 53
Cogswell, LtCdr. James K., 59
Coast Battleship No. 3, 10
Compson, Gen. H. B., 19
Cooper, George, 11
Cooper, Mary Tichenor, 10, 11
crew, in Philippines, *66*; roster, 124ff
Cristobal Colon (Sp. cruiser) 39, 48, 51, 53-
   54, 59, 61; hit, 62; scuttled, 62
Cross, Pvt. Robert, 43-44, 49
Cuba (map), *48*

Davis, Guy A., 95
Davis, Val., 111
Daniels, Josephus (Secy. of Navy), 89
Dewey, Commodore, 37, *60*, 63, 67
Dickens, Capt, Francis W., 74
distances traveled, 41
Douglas, Col., Clarence B., 106
dynamite, 110, 112, 114

Eastwind (USCG Icebreaker), *7*
electric button (launched ship), 19, *20*
Eniwetok Isl., 111
Evans, Capt. (*Iowa*), 53
Evening Journal (newspaper), 58

figurehead, *100; see also:* bow-crest
fire, on *Oregon*, 34
first shot fired in battle, 61, 129
floating ammunition depot, 110n
Foster, Sam., 81
Furor (Sp. torpedo boat), 48; sunk, 62

Galapagos Isl, 64
gangplank, *96*, 98
Gannon, Joseph C., 47, 49n
Golden Gate, 132; (map), *81*
Graves, Gen. Wm. S., 86
guillotine, 20ı
Guantanamo Bay (map), *48*
"guest list" *see:* passenger

Gulf of Pechili (China), 69, *70*

Havana, Cuba (map), *48*
Hawthorne Bridge (Portland), 93
Hearst, Wm. Randolph, 13, 14n, 15, 29, 50, *53*, 58-59
Hegira (ship), 96
Heiser, Victor, MD, 64n
Hiroshima, Japan, 71, 72
Historical Society of Vermont, 84
Hobbs, Patricia A., 12
Hong Kong, 60, 67, 74
Honolulu, Hawaii, 67
Hopegh Sound, China, 69
Howison, Capt. Henry L., 23
Howki Lighthouse, 69
Hudson River parade, 7, *56, 57*
Hughes, Hon. C. E., 91
Hughes, RAdm., C. F., 133

Indiana (battleship), 17, 41, 52, 57, 89
Infanta Maria Teresa, see: Maria Teresa
Iris (distillery ship), 64n, 67
Iwai Sanggo Co. (Japan), 115
IX-22, 109, 110

Japanese (soldiers), 111
Jenson, Cdr. Henry N., 78
Jupiter Inlet, 32, 41
Justin (collier), 64

Kawasaki, Japan, 115
Kempff, Adm. Louis, 69
Kent, David A., 12, 118
Key West, 38, 39, 40
King, Lt. Frank R., 78
Kure Naval Shipyard (Japan), 69, 71, 72, 83; repair fails, 74

Lane, Gen. Joseph, 19
Lang, Cdr. Charles J., 78
last shot fired, 61
launches, steam, *35*, 36
Liberty ships, 109
Liberty Ship Park, *106*
Lima, Peru, 31
Lord, Gov., 26
Lukens, Leonard, 12

maps, *32, 48, 70, 80*
mahogany (pilot house), 38
Maine, 9, 13, 14, 15, 29, 60, 61
Manila Bay, Philippine Isl, 60, 67
Mare Island Navy Yard, 75, *76*
Maria Teresa (Sp. cruiser) 48, *52*; -burned, beached, 62
Merrimak, 42
Marietta (gunboat), 31, 35, 36, 37, 38

Marines (roster), 129; tribute to, *104*
Marshall Isl., 111
Martinique, 39; (map), *32*
Massachusetts (battleship), 557, 89
Massey Supply Co., 114
Meriso, Guam, 111-114, 130
Merrell, Capt. John P., 84
Mike Laudenklos (fireboat), 96
Milligan, Ch.Engr. Robert W., 34, 49, 53
Monadnock (monitor), 26
Monterey (monitor), 26
Montevideo, Uruguay, 64
Morro Castle, Cuba, 44; (map), *48*
Mulkey (patrol boat), 94
Myers, capt. John T., 69
Myerson, James P., 12

McCracken, LtCdr. Alexander, 67
McCormick, Capt. Alexander, 29
McKinley (Pres.) Wm. 13, 14

National Encampment United States Veterans of the Span-Amer War, 93
Navy League, 102
Newark (cruiser), 69
New York (cruiser), 44, 49, 69
Nictheroy (cruiser), 36, 37, 38

Olympia (cruiser), 17, 23, 37, 60
Oregon Steam navigation Company, 18
Oregon Journal (newspaper), 93-94
Oquando (Sp. cruiser), 21n, 48, *50*, 51; wrecked, *50* burned, beached, 62
O'Shea Pvt. Joseph H., 48, 61, 129
Owens, LtCdr., Charles T., 78

Palau Isl, 112
Panama-Pacific Int'l Exposition, 79, *80*
parade, Hudson River, *56, 57*
Paragua (gunboat), 67
passengers (list), 94, *95*
pennant, *92*
Pennoyer, Gov. Sylvester, 19
Philippine Isl, 84, 118
Pittman, Gilbert, 12
Pluton (Sp. torpedo boat), 48, 50; sunk, 62
Po Hai, China, 69
Portal, Richard, 11
Portland (tugboat), 96
postmarks, *108, 117, 118, 119, 120, 121*
post offices on *Oregon*; *see*: postmarks
Presidio of San Francisco (map), *80*, 135
Public Market moorage, 94
Puget Sound Navy Yard, *75*, 77, 78, 88, 133
Pulitzer, Joseph, 13, 15
Punta Arenas, Chili, 7, 35, 41, 64, 121; (map), *32*

140

Raby, LtCdr. James J., 78
radio, 65
radio shack, *108*
Ramsay, Sgt. Fred A., 61, 98
red ribbon (arm band), 38
Richards, Leverett, 86n
Rio de Janeiro, Brazil, 36, 64, 121; (map), *32*
Rogers, Cdr. R. R., 87
Roosevelt, Theodore, 14n
Roosevelt, Franklin D., 91; Pres. 93, 109
Rose Festival, (Portland), 99
Rowan, Lt. Andrew S., 10, 135

St. Paul (cruiser), 43
Samar (gunboat, 67
Sampson, Adm. Wm. T., 40, 44-45. *60*
Sandy Point, Chili, 32
San Francisco, Calif. (map), *80*
San Juan Hill, Cuba, *48*
Santiago de Cuba, 52; (map), *48*
Schley, Adm, Winfield Scott, 42, 45n, 49, 51, 52, 57, *60*
Schminck Memorial Museum, *107*
Scandia (collier), 63
Scott, Irving, 18
Scranton, Lt. Edison E., 78
searchlights, 36, 43, 89, *99*, 113
Shelby, Eugenia, 19, 20
Siapan Isl., 112
Siberia, 86
Siboney, Cuba, 44
silver service, *25*, 26
Smith, Bridget E., 12
Sousa, John Phillip, *55*
souvenirs, 78, *88*, *107*
Spanish cruisers (listed), 48
Spectator (newspaper), 93
Sprague, Gov. Charles A., 109
Star-Bulletin (newspaper), 115
Statue of Liberty, 59
Steel Bridge (Portland), 94
Stevens, Willard H., 98
Straight, Mary Beth, 11
Strait of Juan de Fuca, 23, 78
Strait of Magellan, 33, 34, 41, 63, 64, 98, 132; (map), *32*
Subic Bay, Philippines, 68

Taku, China (map), 69, *70*
Temerario (Sp. destroyer), 33, 35
Texas (cruiser), 42, 49, *56*, 89
Thomas, Capt. Charles M., 74, 121
Thompson, Cora A., 90
Tichenor, Capt. Wm., 10
Tichenor, Mary Walker, 10, 11
Tinian Isl., 112

Topete, RAdm. Pascual Cervera y, 37
Tracy, Gen. B. F., 17
Travis, Sgt. Robert W., 86n
Tsukuduo, Adm. Tatsuo, 11-12, 71
typhoon, 75, 114

Union Iron Works, 18, 19, 23, 130
Urdaneta (gunboat), 67
USAT Thomas (troop transport), 86
USS Caelum (freighter), 111
USS Constitution 17
USS Memphis (cruiser), 119
USS Missouri (battleship), *112*
USS LCI(G)-474, 111
USS Idaho (battleship), 89
USS Iowa (battleship), 49, 52, 57, 63
USS Mississippi (battleship), 89
USS New Mexico (battleship), 89
USS North Carolina, 119
USS Oregon, after battle, *vi*; armament on, 21; arr at Santiago, 41; at Astoria, 78, *81*, at Guam, *112*, *113*, *115*; constr approved, 17; cost of, 21; deck, *66*; disabled by treaty, 134; drawing of, 29; fires first and last shots in battle, 61; grounded, 69, *70*; in Hudson River, *56*, *57*; in three wars, *ii*, 10; launched, 19, 20; its power, 23; scrapped, 115, *116*; sea trials, 23, *27*, *28*, *29*; shoots *Colon*, 62; service medals earned, 116
USS Vicksburg (Gunboat), 86
Universal Ship Cancellation Society, 12

Valparaiso, Chili, 64
Veterans of Foreign Wars, 94, 98
Vigan, Philippine Isl, 67-68
Viscaya (Sp. cruiser), 48, 51; burned, beached, 62
Vladivostok, 86

Washington Naval Treaty, 91, 109, 134
Webber, Bert, 12, 101, *135*, 136,
Webber, Lauren, *105*
Webber, Margie, 136
Webber, Richard, E., *7*
Wilde, Capt., 67, 74
Willamette River, 92, *95*, *96*,99, 100, 102, 110
Williams, Cdr., G. W., 79
Wilmington (cruiser)m 40
Wilson, Edith Boling, 89
Wilson, Pres. Woodrow, 12, 88-89

Yokohama, Japan, 69, 83, 116